TRANSFORM YOUR COMMUNICATION SKILLS

STEVE BRIDGER

Matador
9 Priory Business Park,
Wistow Road, Kibworth Beauchamp,
Leicestershire. LE8 0RX
Tel: (+44) 116 279 2299
Fax: (+44) 116 279 2277
Email: books@troubador.co.uk
Web: www.troubador.co.uk/matador

ISBN 978 1784624 996
eISBN 978 1784626 624

British Library Cataloguing in Publication Data.
A catalogue record for this book is available from the British Library.

Printed and bound by CPI Group (UK) Ltd, Croydon, CR0 4YY
Typeset in 11.5pt Gill Sans Light by Troubador Publishing Ltd, Leicester, UK

Matador is an imprint of Troubador Publishing Ltd

MIX
Paper from
responsible sources
FSC® C013604

This book is dedicated to the wonderful E.L.B.
without whom there would be no S.P.B.

SPECIAL THANKS FOR THEIR EXPERT COLLABORATION, IN CHAPTER ORDER, GO TO:

Stephen Engwell:	https://www.linkedin.com/in/stephenengwell
Sally Hindmarch & Annie Farr:	partnerswithyou.co.uk
Peter Cooke:	dudleighfilms.com
Steve Hyland & Linda Bazant:	businessconnectionslive.com
Mark Hughes:	threetiermedia.com
Melonie Dodaro:	topdogsocialmedia.com
Jonathan L. Davey:	theberkshireblog.com
Steve Preston:	smp-solutions.co.uk

Permissions:

Tapping Image with kind permission from www.thrivingnow.com

'We're Prepared' Scout Image with permission from the State Library of South Australia

'Salvador Dali' Photo Editorial Credit: Toniflap/Shutterstock.com

Thanks to:

Deepa Veneik of Surbiton Law, Ruth Fogg of Stressworx and Mark Brewer of Balance Rite Osteopathy for their support, and to Carla Terrell of Ashburn, Virginia USA.

CONTENTS

SECTION THREE – WRITING SKILLS 137

SECTION FOUR – REFERENCE SECTION 205

TRANSFORM YOUR COMMUNICATION SKILLS SPEAK, WRITE, PRESENT WITH CONFIDENCE

Introduction

Where this book will take you

Improving your speaking, writing and presenting skills will accelerate your career and become a valuable asset in your business and personal life.

Armed with the contents of these pages, you'll quickly reap the benefits of being more confident, more skilful and become the creator of highly effective communications. The quality of your speaking and writing will deliver professional and personal rewards. The contents of this book, with practice and dedication, will transform your skills and deliver long-term benefits.

The Approach

This book is intended to be a practical, everyday resource, an easily digestible reference guide. Proven techniques and insights are shared to make an immediate impact and improve performance at whatever point you've reached.

The Collaboration Effect

Transform Your Communication Skills has been written with the collaboration of talented specialists who pass on their knowledge gained from years of running their own businesses. This real-life learning provides a useful source of practical help rather than pages of baffling theory. Let me introduce the team as they appear in chapter order.

Stephen Engwell, NLP Master Practitioner

Steve is a consultant and NLP (Neuro Linguistic Programming) Master Practitioner providing coaching therapy to help change people's lives for the better. His advice will constructively modify behaviour to manage nerves and improve presentation performance. Meet Steve in Chapter 5 and again in Chapter 7.

Sally Hindmarch, Managing Director, and Annie Farr, Actor and Trainer, at Partners with You

Partners with You use the skills professional actors learn in drama school to transform the presentation capabilities of people in business. Sally contributes exercises and techniques to help you look, sound and feel confident in speaking whether it's a one-to-one encounter in the office or standing in front of many faces staring up at you. Annie Farr is a professional actor with theatre, TV and film credits to her name. Annie is Sally's principal workshop leader. Learn from Sally and Annie in Chapters 7 and 8.

Peter Cooke, Managing Director of Dudleigh Films

Peter studied at the London Academy of Media, Film and Television. He brings fresh creativity to filmmaking, including business, corporate, property, event and music videos. Peter will explain how to prepare and present videos for business purposes. Get Peter's advice on how to create a great video impression in Chapter 9.

Steve Hyland and Linda Bazant, Managing Directors of Business Communications Live and Retail Therapy Television

Steve and Linda have many years' experience in TV production and media training. Their guidance is especially valuable for media situations on radio and television. Improve your performance in front of the microphone or camera with Steve and Linda in Chapter 10.

Mark Hughes, Social Media Specialist and Co-founder of Three Tier Media

Mark is a talented social media marketing trainer. His approach de-mystifies and quickly shows ways to make the most of social media. Mark will explain the Five Cornerstones of social media in Chapter 12, where he will be joined by Melonie Dodaro, a social media expert from Canada.

Melonie Dodaro, International #1 Bestselling Author of *The LinkedIn Code*, LinkedIn Expert, Keynote Speaker, and Social Selling Evangelist from Kelowna, British Columbia, Canada

Melonie has written an article on social media etiquette. It concentrates on LinkedIn, the international business networking portal. Her advice provides valuable guidance on how to be seen as someone who really knows how to show respect and consideration online.

Jonathan L. Davey, Network Development Specialist

Jon is an expert on creating and managing a business network. He has contributed a piece on the role of newsletters to build your business and, importantly, to interact and contribute to the local community too. His energies have resulted in his business network providing help for good causes around the world. You'll find Jon in Chapter 14.

Steve Preston, Managing Director of SMP Solutions Career & People Development Consultancy

Steve is a career coach and author of *Winning through Redundancy*. He created the '6 Step Change Cycle' to help people develop their business careers and often to reshape their wider ambitions in life too. Steve contributed his experience in the 'How to Write a Case Study' section in Chapter 17.

Steve Bridger, Business Author, Novelist and Business Coach

My background spans advertising, integrated marketing and copywriting. I am the author of **Success before Start-Up**, a pre start-up book. My novel is **One Degree North**, an action thriller set in Singapore in the 1960s. I'm also a business start-up coach. I'm proud to be working with Surrey University and running seminars at the City of London Business Library. My entrepreneurial experience has been in setting up my own small business in gardening, 'Spanish Rings', are Spanish-style flower pot holders. Please visit: www.spanishrings.com.

OUR AIM

We will help you:

- Gain the career and ultimately life-long value of improved personal communication skills
- Become a confident speaker
- Learn how to craft effective written communications
- Manage nerves and channel them to perform well in presentations.

Together, we'll take 3 steps.

STEP 1
THE BEGINNING

Learn how to:

1. Visualise what it will be like when you become a confident speaker, writer and presenter
2. Appreciate the key elements that speaking and writing have in common
3. Understand the particular dynamics of communicating in a business situation
4. Consider the best times in the working day for you to prepare and to perform
5. Memorise the Golden Rules of speaking and writing
6. Prepare and structure a presentation
7. Analyse an audience and pitch at the right level with the right content
8. Connect with an audience and individuals within an audience
9. Create a confident elevator pitch (a one-minute mini-presentation).

STEP 2
SPEAKING AND PRESENTATION SKILLS

Learn how to:

1. Gain confidence and manage your nerves
2. Control your voice and use breathing exercises to look and sound professional
3. Prepare and deliver a speech for a business or personal occasion
4. Prepare for media interviews or for appearances on audio or video
5. Present online using video
6. Prepare and deliver a webinar
7. Understand the etiquette of social media messages.

STEP 3
WRITING SKILLS

Learn how to:

1. Write for your reader
2. Structure a document and write meeting minutes
3. Write press releases and newsletters
4. Write emails and avoid common mistakes
5. Structure and write business case studies
6. Write a memorable and effective CV, resume or one-pager.

A Fourth Element

At the end of the book you'll find a reference section that covers punctuation and has an A-Z of useful terms, just to provide a little more brain food.

Let's begin.

SECTION 1

GENERAL
COMMUNICATION
SKILLS

THE IMPORTANCE OF THE COMMUNICATOR

Imagine this:

Pretend for a moment that you are a fly on the wall looking down on a busy office. The sales people are burning up the phones, the accountants are sinking under a mountain of spreadsheets. The production department are going ballistic as a machine has broken down. Stress reigns.

You are sitting alone ready to speak, ready to deliver important news. Shortly they will all stop and you'll be the centre of attention. Why are you so calm?

The answer:

You've worked hard on communication skills and know this is not about you as an individual; not about the way you look, the clothes you wear, no, this is about the content of the message you're about to deliver. The pressure and nerves are eased because you know it's not personal. You've managed to lift and separate your innermost thoughts and feelings. It's the message that matters. Realising this is so IMPORTANT. It takes the weight off you personally and places it on the work you are about to do. You've got the balance right and defused your nerves.

Good communicators are judged by the results they achieve through helping others. Success is judged by getting others to:

- Fully comprehend your meaning
- Take the action you've described
- Achieve the outcomes you've set.

Business communication is not Shakespeare. Flowery prose or soaring oratory is not necessary. Here are three watchwords that lay the foundations for effective communication:

PURPOSE – CLARITY – BREVITY

1. **Purpose**
   'Begin with the end in mind' – Stephen R Covey

As a messenger you have two sets of goals, running parallel. One is to create a compelling piece of communication that is fully understood by the audience. The second is to consider how best to present the message effectively and how to put it across.

Setting goals requires you to define your purpose. What do you want to achieve?

Why are you doing this?

- To inform – to spread news
- To educate – to train colleagues – to improve capabilities
- To sell – to persuade, to argue your case, to generate physical sales
- To brief – to get others to perform a task
- To instruct – to pass on management decisions – to request action
- To motivate – to encourage and reward
- To praise – to recognise achievement
- To discipline – to maintain respect and improve relationships
- To gain feedback – to learn people's views
- To ask for co-operation and involvement
- To gather information

Once you've set your goals the next task is to pitch the content at the right level. Shortly you will learn how to analyse audience characteristics in order to set the right tone of voice and delivery style. By understanding the composition of the audience you can shape the message to gain acceptance of your proposals.

2. Clarity

There's nothing worse than sitting in a presentation where the speaker assumes too much knowledge or disregards the audience altogether. How many times have you sat and listened, trying to understand, but have been disregarded by a self-absorbed speaker?

The tell-tale signs are the presenter:

- Using words and phrases that show how clever they are
- Using acronyms without bothering to explain what the acronym letters stand for
- Using jargon that is understood by only a few.

Your aim is always to be inclusive in your delivery and ensure that people are clear about what you want to say. The central purpose is to enlighten, energise and maybe amuse and entertain. Business is not meant to be dull and boring. It's been proven that people learn quicker when relaxed and receptive. They are more open to learning. Capturing attention, holding attention and achieving the result is testament to your role and talent as a communicator.

3. Brevity

Everyone is busy; deadlines to meet, meetings to attend, issues to be resolved, busy, busy, busy. The more you can do to discipline your presentation or written document the better. This calls for dedicating sufficient time beforehand to drafting your document or scripting a speech. The golden rule in writing a document is to make sure it 'stands alone' and is written in a way that doesn't need you to be there to explain it. Often documents are left for others to read without the benefit of hearing your rationale in person.

To recap Stephen Covey's words, 'Begin with the end in mind.'

1. Visualise your ideal outcomes.
2. Make sure your message is clear and unambiguous – simple language, short sentences.

3. Keep it tight and to the point.
4. Define your call to action or specify the next steps and specify timelines.

COMMUNICATION ELEMENTS COMMON TO BOTH SPEAKING AND WRITING

A quick recap of what we've covered so far:

- By its nature, communication must be designed to further the development and smooth running of the organisation or educate or inspire an audience; ideally all three.
- Communication must reach out and involve all parties with clear comprehension and set goals.
- Being inclusive, communication must motivate and meet the commercial needs of the organisation in all its different aspects and be suited to all levels of management.

Transmitting and Receiving

In short, communicators have to ensure that there are no potential misunderstandings contained in the messages they're transmitting by voice or writing. Communicators need to check that, once transmitted, their messages have been received and actioned correctly. Communication through the spoken or written word have elements in common.

1. Write for the Reader

Writing is a personal one-to-one experience. Ninety-nine percent of the time, you're making contact with one other human being at one moment in time, even though what you've written may have a circulation list, only one pair of eyes is reading at any one time.

This means you must consider the nature, status and role of the person who will be reading your piece and write accordingly. Write in a way that will make them feel like you are talking to them and them alone. This goes back to the advice at the very beginning of the book. Effective results are achieved by considering the reader or listener before you lift a pen or strike the computer keyboard because your job is to make sure they understand and take the action you want them to take.

To do this you need to:

- Choose the most appropriate language, using words and phrases carefully chosen and grammatically correct
- Address them in keeping with their status; if you're writing a report to be read by senior management it has to be professional and follow conventional, accepted norms of address and content presentation
- Use a tone of voice that is in keeping with the nature of your message, perhaps more relaxed and informal for fellow workers, more formal for senior management
- Ask yourself whether your work will be for internal consumption or for those outside your business
- If you're writing to gain commitment or ask someone to do something, use words or phrases that suit the people you're trying to persuade
- Remember that any forms of business communication, either spoken or written, are parts of an ongoing process, not a one-off function. It's a good idea to ask for feedback to make people feel they can query

or clarify points they may not be clear about and, importantly, to show that you will be receptive and welcome comment

- Be aware of any particular pressures, stresses or operational situations that may affect the ability or preparedness of people to do what you ask. This is where your interpersonal and diplomatic skills come in.

2. Speak to and for the Listener

An accomplished communicator thinks about educating and informing *for* the benefit of the listener. Clearly the obvious difference between speaking and writing is that when speaking the receiver of the message is standing right in front of you. You can see who they are and by reading the visual signals you can decide on how to put your message across. The visual signals may include the way they're dressed, formally or casually, their age and gender, and it may be possible to sense their mood, whether they are in a generally positive or negative frame of mind, from their expression. Speaking to one person whom you may know takes the guesswork out of your approach. You can feel more comfortable about the tone of voice and, using tact and diplomacy, choose a delivery style that will resonate with them.

How well do you know yourself?

You've been reading these first few pages with your thinking head on. You've engaged your brain, now take a moment to engage the rest of your body.

Have you thought how you can improve your own personal communication performance by working to the rhythms of your own mind and body? You can work smarter, be more productive, more successful if you harness your talent and play to your natural strengths, strengths that connect to the time of your working day. Generally people fall into one of two camps.

Are You a Lark or an Owl?

Larks are morning people. They fizz with energy and they're at their brightest and bubbliest up to the middle of the day. Owls are the reverse, they slowly gather momentum throughout the day and the afternoon and evening are their prime times.

As communicators, larks should perform in the morning, the best time of the day for them. If possible, they should arrange meetings and presentations when they are mentally and physically fresh. Afternoons are the time to research and prepare. Owls are wired the other way round. Which camp do you fall into? You will find that by thinking and planning your day you'll get very good at channelling your talents to the greatest effect and achieve the most gratifying results.

2

PREPARING A PRESENTATION

Develop Structure and Content

It's easy to become overwhelmed by the sheer size of a project or the thought of preparing an important presentation. Have you heard of the Russian dolls approach to problem solving? The idea is to down-size big issues into smaller, more manageable sections. This will reduce an intimidating proposition into its component parts and reduce the fear factor.

This is how the idea works in practice. To begin you have one large Russian doll. This doll represents a big issue or in our case the whole task of preparing a presentation from scratch. To make the project manageable the big project needs to be reduced into its component parts; in this illustration, the progressively smaller Russian dolls you find inside one another within the body of the first big doll. Once a presentation is deconstructed it can be approached one step at a time and completed in a more manageable sequence. Look at the picture and commit it to memory. Knowing how you can break down a project could stop you having a breakdown!

The Presentation Preparation Process

Presentations come in all shapes and sizes, including:

* Unexpected encounters where you meet someone of importance and you have to immediately respond to questions in a coherent and intelligent way on the spot
* Networking events where you're given a short time, perhaps only one minute, to deliver an introduction to yourself and your business
* Small group or team meetings where you know the participants and have time to prepare
* Larger gatherings where you do not know all the members
* Set-piece presentations for sales meetings or other company events
* Speaking to strangers lucidly – either people within your organisation or external contacts.

Where to start?

Obviously, preparing a presentation comes before delivering it. This section contains advice on preparation of the material itself and the audiovisual aids needed to deliver it. This does not go into presentation software or techy details, only the principles of preparation.

You can apply the 80:20 principle to presentations. According to this principle,

80% of the time would be spent in creating and developing the presentation and 20% in the delivery. When it comes to the delivery stage, when you're happy with the content, the same principle drives the rehearsal time. Eighty percent of the time would be dedicated to rehearsal and 20% to the final performance.

In a normal business scenario, your boss would have briefed you on the purpose and objective of the presentation. These are not necessarily one and the same thing. You could have a quantified business objective of, for example, increasing sales by 2% or gaining distribution of 10% in a new territory, but the purpose of the presentation would be to inspire or motivate or educate the audience on what their part is in the campaign, to explain their roles in the proceedings and describe the sales and marketing support they'll receive to ultimately achieve the key financial objectives.

It is vital to give people time to focus on you and the presentation and forget about their other responsibilities for the short time they're with you. Briefly outlining the purpose of the meeting, the ground you'll cover, the expected length of time it will take and your decision as to where and when questions will be addressed buys time for your workmates to leave their issues outside the door and engage with you.

Structuring a Conventional Presentation

You would hopefully expect colleagues to participate positively in the process as the success of the company should benefit them and for them to be keen to contribute and share their expertise to further improve initiatives. While the whole presentation is of interest to everyone, as a presenter you need to pay particular attention to providing solid evidence and support for the main proposition.

Here's a 4-part structure guide.

1. Introduction

- Introduce yourself and your role within the company.
- Explain what the presentation is about and what you will be covering.
- Stress the relevance of the presentation to your audience or reader and how they will personally benefit.

2. Background

- Describe the market or commercial situation.
- Outline the business opportunity or reasons for any change or development.
- Describe the desired outcomes.
- Indicate areas of your audience's involvement and contribution.

3. Main Content

- State the presentation objectives.
- Explain the details of the proposition.
- Describe the benefits.
- Show how the proposition will affect them.
- Provide details of how the proposition will be implemented.
- Highlight any issues to be addressed arising from the proposal.

4. Conclusion – Summary and Action Plan

- Summarise the main points.
- Explain the next action steps.
- Take questions from the floor and invite discussion.
- Gain feedback on the meeting. Encourage audience participation to suggest any improvements.
- Invite anyone who has further questions or wants clarification to meet with you after the presentation or at a later date.
- Supply contact details.
- Leave copies of related documents or information sheets.

Here's a reference template as a reminder:

Core Element	Content
1. Introduction It's most important to set the scene and state that supporting information is available to be taken away. This will demonstrate you have done your homework and prepared properly for the needs of the audience members.	Presentation Name Purpose of presentation Briefly describe the content order Availability of presentation notes or charts Availability of supporting research or evidence Approximate presentation running time Questions during or time at the end?
2. Background to the presentation subject	Describe commercial opportunity, competitive environment, reason for this session
3. Presentation Objective	What's the purpose – new product launch? Product development? Structural change? Entering new market? Training Programme?
4. Main Proposition	Describe gains and benefits then quantify and provide figures, summarise key results of research
5. Implementation Plans	Give timing and resource requirements (people, money, materials). Highlight any anticipated issues, obstacles to be overcome.
6. Summary and Next Steps	Recap on key points and assign responsibilities for tasks that need to be accomplished by given dates.
7. Questions and possible discussions	Give out supporting information to participants. If questions from the floor cannot be answered, state when you will respond with the answers.

Dance with the Devil – It's not over when it's over

It's not over when you've finished preparing your presentation. The last step is to dance with the devil. The devil's not just in the detail but lurking in the core content too. Before you turn your attention to delivering a presentation you must:

- Read and re-read your piece to make sure nothing is missing. Frequently, it's what you've forgotten that catches you out
- When you've finished the first draft, walk away. Leave it overnight and read it again with fresh eyes the next morning. Often you will see things clearly after taking a break
- Ask someone else to read it and give it a negative critique. Ask them to find fault and challenge your approach so you can see your work dispassionately. Make sure you do this with time to make any corrections or add anything missed. Hopefully they will compliment you if your work passes the test
- Make sure your work is grammatically correct with no spelling mistakes
- Make doubly sure that you only use jargon or acronyms or business terms that everyone understands. It's your responsibility to make sure they do. If not sure, check and explain or avoid such terms altogether. To show consideration for your audience you can follow the same practice as you would when writing by saying out loud what the letters of an acronym mean in the context of the presentation, for example, KPI may stand for Key Performance Indicator or Key Person of Influence. The audience will thank you
- Challenge your own thinking and try to anticipate areas of presentation weakness. By following this process you can identify areas that could be questioned by your audience. This will give you time to prepare answers for those **What if** speculations that come particularly from the questioners. This is when you become a questioner and look for weak spots
- Realise that part of the process is anticipating audience reaction and pinpoint areas open to question. One way to do this is to think about audience members not according to their personality traits but as colleagues and individuals. As you know them personally or about them

by reputation, you can be pretty sure of their area of interest and imagine the kind of questions they may ask or clarification they may seek

- Research, write and commit to memory your answers to anticipated questions so you can be ready to respond. If you do not know an answer, say you don't know and say when you will be back with an answer. DO NOT allow awkward moments to derail the rest of your presentation or all your good work will be undone
- Finally on this row of bullet points, commit yourself to learning the content of your presentation to make it a part of you, embedded in your brain.

NAILING THE ELEVATOR PITCH
THE 60-SECOND PRESENTATION

How long is a minute? Solve the Riddle of Time

Don't you hate being unexpectedly put on the spot? It can happen at any time in your working week. You're getting on with your job and suddenly someone stops you to ask who you are, what you're doing and why? Or have you been at a conference or seminar or at a business networking session where you have to stand up to introduce yourself and your business and given only one minute to say something that is coherent without your brain freezing and your tongue being tied in knots?

Apparently the elevator pitch was so called by Michael Caruso when he was editor of *Vanity Fair* magazine. He had experienced a series of chance encounters when time was limited and facts had to be shared succinctly, professionally and successfully. The idea was that you had to be prepared to give essential information about yourself, your business or a proposition in the time it took for an elevator to ride between floors or complete its rise or descent; this ranged from thirty seconds to three minutes.

One or two minutes are the most common timings. Wouldn't it be brilliant to prepare a mini-presentation **before** you are caught in the corridor by the managing director or **before** your name is called to stand up and talk? Wouldn't it be really helpful to map out in advance a speech of five or ten minutes long?

How do you solve the riddle? Think sideways. Think in a different way.

The key to unlocking the mystery is to think about time in a different way. Not in seconds, minutes or hours but in terms of what you can accomplish in a given time span. How many cups of coffee can you drink at your desk in a morning? How many paperclips do you use in a day? How many miles per hour? The answer is not MPH but WPM. How many Words per Minute can you speak?

The answer is approximately 120 to 160 words per minute, depending on your speed of delivery. Those figures solve the riddle of the sands. By knowing how many words you can speak you can slice one minute into neat parcels of time and relevant pieces of information. You can follow this template as a starting point.

The 60-Second Template – A Guide to Successful Business Speed Pitching

You can shape the content and timing to fit your message. Use this guide to get you started by writing down what you want to say in a structured way. Time yourself as you speak the words to see how it suits your speed and style of delivery. As a rough guide you can say two words every second. Here are two scenarios to in which to apply the technique.

1. A 60-Minute Business Introduction

Content Suggestion	Seconds	Word Count
Your name, status, company name	10	20
What does your company do? What's your role in the company? What function do you perform?	15	30
What are the unique selling points? What makes your company different? What brands or products are you known for?	20	40
Are there any new products/ special offers or any newsworthy achievements?	10	20
Ask for business cards and give them yours. Suggest a meeting – put their number on your phone. Arrange a personal meeting.	5	10
Total:	60	120

2. A Business Networking Scenario

Content Suggestion	Seconds	Word Count
Your name, status, company name and what you do	10	20
What is your company known for reputation wise? Quality of products and service	15	30
Your special skills/experience/unique selling points/testimonials/integrity and quality	15	30
What kind of business leads or referrals are you looking for?	10	30
Reprise name and contact details or arrange a meeting.	5	10
Total	60	120

Be Fresh and Creative

These templates give you a starting point. The main thing is to marshal your information then prioritise what you want to say. Be careful to structure your pitch and devote the right combination of words and time to each aspect to be covered. Once you've had a first stab at it speak at your normal speed and time yourself. You can then make adjustments to bring you close to the time limit, allowing for pauses. Silence is extremely effective too, to accentuate a point. You can then print it to read to people or commit it to memory. It's a good idea to refresh your text to include new developments in your business or to pick up on any items in the local or national news that you can link to your piece.

Networking Pointers

Networking is all about building trust. By attending a meeting or networking group you are the physical representation of your business. This is an immediate, positive point in a world where people buy people and the human factor is of immense importance. However, you must avoid the biggest mistake of all by adopting a hard-sell attitude. You have to gain the confidence of others before they will readily accept you and your business. Also, one thing to learn is not to talk endlessly about what you do and what you as a business are capable of. It's not only about what you can do, it's about what you can do for them. How you can bring value or help their business either with something solid in product terms or, most helpfully, what experience you can share and what advice you can give.

The following points are worth knowing to help you become successfully active in networking:

- The emphasis on building relationships and trust
- The degree of success depends upon the commitment and quality of the individual: quality of service, expertise and reliability
- Appreciate that willingly sharing your expertise is an important feature of networking
- Networking is about both giving and taking. One networking group uses the term Givers Gain, meaning that people who are generous with their time usually reap the rewards of their actions
- Think about how you can adapt your proposition to solve their needs. How can you make a difference to them?

Here are a couple of real 60-second pitches with kind permission from Deepa Veneik of Surbiton Law and Mark Brewer of Balance-Rite Osteopathy. They show that you can communicate a lot of information in just one minute. You can speak these examples out loud and time them:

'Good morning, I am Deepa Veneik, a lawyer with Surbiton Law LLP.
There are three things you should know about Surbiton Law.
First: We are based – guess where – Surbiton!
Second: We offer expert, no nonsense and constructive legal advice to business.
Third: We provide a residential property and domestic conveyancing service.
Now for some detail; as business people, you or someone you may know could need this kind of contribution such as help on Employment Law and advice on general matters of Business Law – for example, contracts, IT Law and Intellectual Property Rights.
Surbiton Law gives you advice you can trust. Talk to us. We're here to protect your interests.
Word Count: 108

Mark Brewer of Balance-Rite Osteopathy
'Hello, my name is Mark Brewer. I'm from the Balance-Rite Osteopathy Clinic.
I offer a service where I diagnose and care for your bodily aches and pains. Whether they are due to sporting activities or caused by other medical conditions, I provide natural and effective treatment.
This is achieved by providing a total-body treatment, which aims to relax and restore mobility, and balances the body structures that have gone off the rails and have become dysfunctional.
I know that osteopathy can benefit everyone, whether with back pain, for prevention, or for better overall health.
Please refer people who need advice and treatment to come and see me at our new premises in Chertsey.
I'm Mark Brewer of Balance-Rite Osteopathy.'
Word Count: 120

3. A Personal Introduction.

You've seen how important building trust and creating relationships is in networking. Creating your own personal version of the 60-second elevator technique will stand you in good stead in a job interview situation or in your private life in social gatherings. By thinking about this before you are asked you will be primed and ready to offer a positive human dimension to your business persona. In interviews this aspect is crucial to allow would-be employers to get a feeling for how you would fit in and how your personality would be a great addition to their team. In social gatherings you can introduce humour and originality to the mix too, especially if there's someone special you want to impress.

3

AUDIENCE ANALYSIS AND HOW TO PITCH YOUR MESSAGE

How do you prepare to address a diverse group of people? Your audience may comprise of different levels of seniority, different skills and specialities within an organisation. How do you face five, twenty or a hundred people and say something that will first capture and then keep their attention?

Profiling your Audience – Understand the key personality traits and how to pitch to them

We're all the same, yet very different. That's the puzzle. Your audience may work for the same company, have the same team goals, be working for the same success. Yet it would be a big mistake to address them all in the same manner. Myers Briggs, Carl Jung and many other deep thinkers have developed ideas on personality traits and psychological profiles. There are many views on this subject that delve into great depth but from our practical viewpoint of effectively communicating to a business audience we need to keep the message as manageable as possible for us as transmitters and our audience as receivers. By dividing the audience into three key personality groups that broadly share the same characteristics you can satisfy most of the people most of the time.

The Three Main Profiles

These are the three primary personality traits relevant to the communicator. You may be able to place your colleagues into these broad categories.

First
Big-picture, creative thinkers whose first reaction is to get excited about ideas; these are: *The Visionaries*.

Second
The energetic people who get things done and make things happen these are the doers, the multi-taskers; these are: *The Dynamos*.

Third

The interrogators; these are the doubters. They want convincing. They demand supporting evidence. These are: *The Questioners*.

This segmentation is gold to a communicator. Each of these groups has to be approached in a different way. By knowing the right buttons to push you'll get the reaction you want.

Satisfying the expectations of each of these three groups is the secret of successful spoken and written presentations. How do you identify and connect with these three personality groups?

Identifying the Visionaries – The 'Big Ideas' People

These are the people who literally get the big picture, the blue-sky thinkers. They swiftly understand the overall concept. They are creative. They inspire. They're often among the top strategists of the company and are often skilled delegators. Just think of Richard Branson.

Connecting with Visionaries

When addressing the Visionary, the good communicator introduces a concept as a visual picture painted with words and supporting visuals. The opportunity is fully described and focuses on the project benefits. Any business proposal will be explained in general terms and a description given of how it will work. The writer will provide key pieces of information to demonstrate that all the interlocking strands will come together to achieve the stated objective. A plan will be prepared, allocating responsibilities delegated to key players in the organisation.

Identifying the Dynamos – The Driving Force

These are the action figures that drive businesses forward with their energy, determination and ability to get things done. They understand the vision, they appreciate the business benefits. Their talent is making things happen. In business, they operate at all levels of seniority. Dynamos are influential motivators who encourage and manage others to achieve set tasks. Hilary Clinton comes to mind.

Connecting with Dynamos

Dynamos require a full explanation of the proposal – the idea, the practical operational implementation, timetable and costs. The presentation needs to be complete, with benefits and potential drawbacks highlighted for discussion. An assessment of the demands of the project on the business and a timing plan will be key considerations. The style of communication has to be concise, to the point and well argued.

Identifying the Questioners – The Facts and Figures Challengers

The Questioners would be the detailed text of front-page news. This type of person demands full supporting evidence with every detail checked and double checked. These are the 'Devils Advocates' and 'What if' inquisitors. A proposal will need to be thoroughly vetted before it gains their approval. Often they are the subject specialists in finance, logistics, technology or production who are seen to challenge what is being proposed. They challenge to make sure you know what you're talking about.

Connecting with Questioners

Questioners demand a proposal that is thorough, detailed, straight to the point, with no procrastination, no waffle. Questioners expect a well-constructed argument packed with supporting evidence, facts and figures, and back-up is essential. When I say 'back-up', time will be well spent researching any potential drawbacks and preparing a response for each one. Try to anticipate any awkward questions. Criticise the project in your head and prepare a response. Prepare well and you'll perform well. Misjudge this group and you'll be made to feel very small indeed. Importantly, check out any similar projects in the marketplace, be aware of them. Examine any legal or compliance issues, even if you need to engage their help and experience to overcome any potential hurdle.

THE IMPORTANCE OF IDENTIFYING YOUR AUDIENCE

Admittedly the description of these three personality types is simplified, but the underlying points are important. You need to judge and prepare your material to suit your audience. Misjudging your audience could dramatically affect the outcome, for example:

- A presentation to 'The Visionaries' that is unbalanced and packed with details and structural elements more suited to 'The Questioners' may fail to excite visionary thinkers.
- A proposal for 'The Dynamos' that lacks practical operational and executional elements will be considered incomplete and unrealistic.
- A concept for 'The Questioners' using lightweight images and selling language will fail to impress. Your proposal will not be taken seriously without hard facts that are substantiated.

There's one last point about the Questioners. They could save you from making rash decisions. Their perceived negativity could be ultimately positive. By challenging your thinking they could highlight a problem that had not occurred to you. Their questions may prompt you to investigate an issue and reveal underlying problems. They could be your unlikely saviours.

Audience Profile and Action Summary

Character Type	Characteristics	Identifying Traits	Approach
Visionaries	Creative Big Idea, Blue-Sky thinkers Entrepreneurial outlook They see the idea/ concept in action. Comfortable taking responsibility and making leadership decisions	Natural leaders Confident Personable Motivators Delegators Prime movers Forward thinking Provide solutions to overcome obstacles	Present the Big Picture Stress the benefits Demonstrate how it would help the company to move forward/gain a competitive advantage Explain how the aims/objectives will be achieved

Dynamos	Doers Energetic Committed Achievers Power houses Used to high performance, beating targets and making things happen Problem solvers Good team leaders	Highly practical Talented people Good Managers Workaholics Ambitious Great all-rounders Results-driven	Must cover all the bases: aims/purpose, concept, strategy, practicality, capability, timing, budget, benefits How achievable within the time frame?
Questioners	Vital members of a team Experts in their speciality area 'What If' people – They question everything, they insist on accuracy, ultimately supportive when convinced of a proposition	Natural sceptics Interrogators Distrustful, initially negative, Practical and often difficult Love playing Devil's Advocate Ask questions to see what you know	They demand perfection Need all research to be accurate, all details to be double-checked, statements to be supported with evidence

Left-Brain, Right-Brain, Whole-Brain Thinking and the link with Questioners, Visionaries and Dynamos

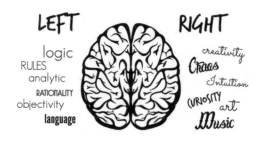

You've probably heard about the supposedly different characteristics of the brain. The idea is that people could be described as left or right brain dominant according to different types of thinking. Left-brain thinkers are supposed to be more logical and analytical while right-brain thinkers are supposedly more creative. From a communicator's viewpoint we do know that our Visionaries display right-hand brain characteristics and the Questioners reveal left-brain tendencies. The Dynamos may occupy the middle ground. Whatever you believe, what is evident is that people do react in different ways.

Satisfying the demands of the three different types in the audience is the challenge. Importantly, breaking down an audience in this way helps you compartmentalise the process to make it easier to tackle. By the way, if at any time you consider starting your own business, think about including people from all three groups in your team. Don't surround yourself with people who will immediately agree with you.

4

PRESENTATION PREPARATION

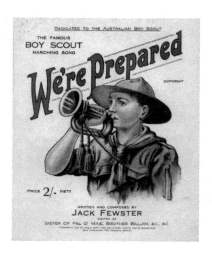

Connecting with and Involving Your Audience

Let's recap on the ground we've covered so far. We've reached Chapter 4 and:

- You know how important you are and the vital role you play as a communicator
- You've understood the particular pressures of a business environment and the need to get your message across in a succinct manner using words and terms that everyone understands
- You've thought about your own brain and body rhythms so you can plan the best time to prepare and the best time to perform
- You learnt how to structure and gather content for a formal presentation and how to prepare and deliver a short, personal mini-presentation for spur-of-the-moment business pitches, networking events and personal

introductions that, prepared properly, can be a good support at job interviews

- You've unlocked the problem of how to analyse and pitch to the three main personality traits in a business situation. Doubtless people could drone on for hours about the whole issue of personality traits but as communicators we need to approach this area with a different outcome in mind. Our priority is to gain the greatest understanding and acceptance from our audience.

The contents of this chapter

When we're at the stage *before* giving the presentation, when we need to think about:

1. What presentation software and any other visual aids you'll use
2. Producing charts that engage and communicate clearly
3. Making sure you've checked the technology and have a back-up plan to avoid techno-disasters
4. Venue Preparation. The physical layout of seats, desks and chairs to suit the subject and occasion
5. Preparing a set of 'house rules' in order that the audience have guidelines on how the presentation will be conducted and your role as presenter, host and event manager
6. Handling hand-outs, when and how to distribute them
7. Distributing or asking people to wear a name tag
8. How to connect with members of the audience on an individual level
9. Strategies to maintain attention. Remembering the 10-Minute Rule of Attention that we'll cover shortly
10. Making sure you regularly check audience understanding
11. Pacing the delivery of the presentation to match the time available
12. Learning how to anticipate and manage interruptions to your flow
13. How to really involve people and encourage their positive participation without letting any one person dominate
14. What you're going to wear. This is more important than you may think.

EVENT PLANNING

1. Using Presentation Software

Let's assume that you're happy with the structure of your presentation and that you've already started to rehearse content. How to deliver your piece effectively is next on the list. Don't be put off by 'Death by PowerPoint'. Audience disengagement occurs when slides become solid with text and used as the presenter's script, or if supporting statistical charts are so congested and dense with detail it is impossible to understand any points being made. If a presenter talks from the slides and not to the audience then death by boredom will surely follow. Beware of over-complication as the human eye and brain need time to sift and absorb information in digestible pieces, so:

- Written slides should use a font style and size that's easy to read
- Any text should be expressed in simple language and short sentences
- Try to use no more than four single-line statements per slide
- A complex message should be broken down over several digestible slides
- The same goes for statistical data; any charts should progressively build and reveal data. It is part of the presenter's job to make sense of the data, share the key points and stress their commercial significance as it relates to the presentation objectives
- Use images and pictures as much as you can. Pictures that relate to the point act as memory hooks for the audience and as visual prompts for the presenter. If the presenter has a print-out of the slides they know in advance the points to be made. As the audience do not know what the picture means until the presenter explains it they will remain engaged. Also, by using pictures and not text slides the audience will not know if a point has been overlooked. By far the best advantage of using images is that you avoid people zoning out of what the presenter is saying because they are too busy reading the slides
- Create your visual presentation to suit your message. Keep it as simple as

possible in case producing a sound and vision extravaganza overshadows or diverts attention

- Produce a single 'blank' slide that reinforces the presentation theme or carries the presentation title. This 'bridging' slide is a visual section break between stages in the presentation. More about the use of this important slide in a moment
- Always assume the worst but hope for the best when it comes to technological gremlins. Take a spare laptop or tablet, projector, connection leads, extension cable and your presentation on two separate USB sticks. Better to be prepared. What do they say – expect the worst and hope for the best?

2. Venue Preparation

Preparing the venue is setting the stage. Considering the physical environment and planning the layout is an indication of how you intend to manage the event and achieve the most positive outcomes.

It also indicates that you are thinking out the nature of the event and your audience. Unless you're giving a keynote speech or talking to people you don't know, the likelihood is that you will be joined by colleagues in a working session. This means the venue is not a classroom and you are not a teacher to be obeyed without question. You need to value their contribution and win their confidence, to persuade rather than dictate. It is not an 'us and them' situation either. You are working for the same company and ultimately have the same goals. This means you are all on the same side and your colleagues should be broadly supportive and want the presentation to go well and have positive results.

Ask yourself:

- What is the expected size of the group?
- Do they need tables or desks in front of them?
- Do you know the expected make-up of the meeting?

35

- What is the nature of the meeting – a training session, a formal briefing, the presentation of a campaign for management approval, a regular weekly performance update?
- What's the best seating layout – semi-circular for a small informal grouping with no hierarchy and everyone together, 'D' shape horseshoe around a boardroom table, angled rows of chairs so people will have an unobstructed view of the screen, or a completely circular set-up to focus attention on any speaker in the middle and for all to have a clear view of the proceedings?
- Do you need to adjust the temperature so people are comfortable but not so hot as to make them fall asleep?
- Is the lighting the right level, not too bright or too dark?
- Is the venue suitable for whose hearing or eyesight is impaired or physically constrained? Are there ramps for wheelchair access or elevators to help people move about as easily as possible?

3. Presentation Management

If you're invited to deliver a keynote speech, give a guest address or to simply stand up and introduce yourself you would not expect audience participation unless you specifically ask for it.

However, the majority of working sessions and project presentations are the opposite. The presenter has to adopt the role of host to guide people through the presentation format as well as delivering the content. The presenter, by walking to the top spot, front and centre of the room, by their body language and saying a few preparatory words, alerts people to the fact that the session is about to start.

To engage attention, explain the content benefits to the audience and reinforce its relevance to them as part of their role in the business.

Presentation Rules

Presentation rules are opening remarks about how the presentation will be conducted. They would cover items such as:

1. Greeting and words of welcome to everyone and mentioning any special guests, for example:
   'Good morning everyone', 'Thanks for being here', 'We'll start in about 5 minutes – before we start I'm going to give you a quick briefing on the presentation format', 'Let me introduce myself, I'll start with a personal introduction'
2. Estimate of the approximate running time
3. Indication of any comfort breaks and when they might be
4. A request to turn all mobiles to silent or off altogether. You could impose a fine with money going to a good cause
5. A request to not concentrate totally on your laptop, iPad or tablet. This is important as involving themselves in their laptops means people are not interacting at the meeting and will probably miss something important
6. A request for people to wear a name tag, normally with their first name written large for easy viewing
7. A decision as to whether questions will be taken during the flow as the presentation progresses, or if time has been allowed for questions at the end. Suggest that people wait a moment before asking a question. Frequently questions relate to the next item you're about to cover
8. The availability of supporting handouts and the timing of their distribution. Most literature is given out after the presentation has ended to avoid people reading the presentation details ahead of the presenter. If you give out copies with charts on one side of the page and space for notes on the other side this can be a useful aid – as long as people don't jump ahead
9. A mention of whether the presentation charts will be available afterwards

10. Indication that you'll meet people after the meeting to discuss any outstanding issues or provide any further clarification. The significance of something so obvious is to underline the fact that communication is an ongoing process, as mentioned before. In writing or speaking, repeating a point helps learning

11. An appreciation that, even with the best will in the world, phones ring, text messages will be read and people will choose to leave the presentation for one reason or another. It's life. Don't let it put you off. If a natural break is not programmed you could say that if people have to leave please could they do so as quickly and as quietly as possible

12. Making the point that you are pleased they attended and welcome their involvement and their contribution.

The Benefits of Setting Presentation Rules

Done carefully and explained as helpful points rather than strict orders, setting presentation rules has a number of positives for the presenter and audience.

For the audience, the time taken on this pre-presentation segment allows their minds to adjust to what is about to happen and leave what has happened either in business or in their private lives outside the room. Setting rules helps them focus on the presenter and presentation.

For the presenter, making these points provides time for nerves to calm down. By explaining the 'rules of engagement' the presenter is taking command. The fact that you are managing the situation professionally, will impress colleagues. As a result, they will pay more attention to your talk. By the time you start your presentation pitch you are mentally ready to go. A good thing to do in these opening remarks is to deliberately slow down your talking speed. Speak slower and breathe deeply to control the rush of adrenalin that kicks in when you first start to speak. Also raise the volume of your voice; how much depends upon the ambient noise in the room. People may be making noise while they find their seats or are speaking to one another. You need to pitch it correctly. Speaking with authority and at a measured pace reinforces your leadership position. By exercising control of your voice you will allow time for your words to come out of your mouth, pass through the air and reach the ears and penetrate the brains of others. There is a time lag. If you talk at speed, it is your nerves talking; slow it down and breathe deeply.

A Final Piece of Pre-prep

Remember the 80/20 rule of the value of proper preparation? Well, there's one last piece of preparation you can do **before** you start to speak, your last piece of research. If you're doing a presentation to work colleagues you already have an advantage. You already know something about them. You know their area of expertise and can judge whether they are people likely to be supportive. At this point you know what you're going to say so you can put these elements together and prepare a selection of questions related to different aspect of the presentation. By having these prepared, it can be just one or two questions; you can pitch them to different people to get approval or affirmation of what you are saying. This is part of the skill of connecting with your audience.

Questions to Break the Ice

Posing questions to the audience that have some relation to the presentation can be a good way to gain knowledge and get their involvement in the very first moments. For example, if you're going to speak about a subject that has recently been on the news you could ask:

Tell me, how many of you saw the TV programme the other night on (linked topic goes here)?'

Or

'I'd like to get to know you a little better, (ask question here).'

4. Connecting with your Audience: Engage – Involve – Enjoy

At first the idea of being able to enjoy presenting may seem a distant hope. You'd be surprised how soon you can edge closer to achieving it. If you remember, we started with the idea that your role as messenger shifts expectations from your shoulders because what you are doing is not about you but about the value of the information you are passing on to others; a gift of knowledge if you like.

Making Personal Contact – Seeing Eye-to-Eye

Smiling, being relaxed and welcoming puts people at ease. The next section of speaking skills will go deeper into this aspect. For now, the important thing is having the confidence to make eye contact with members of the audience; this is not locking stares but seeming to be approachable and sharing, not distant and school-masterly. Making eye contact engages attention and keeps people involved throughout the presentation if you learn to make visual 'sweeps' to include those sitting at the front, back and sides of the room. By looking outward you will also detect whether people are involved and spot those who clearly aren't.

Remember the importance of body language? To make a strong connection with your audience it is vital to get body language right. If you smile, raise your chin to look beyond the front row and scan the room to involve everyone it is a good starting point. Once the presentation is underway, continue to make this visual link. By doing this all audience members will feel you are involving them.

When it comes to addressing a particular person in the audience, use your body to project visual evidence that you are listening. Nodding your head, making open-palmed movements with your hands, raising your eyebrows and making suitably encouraging facial expressions underscores the spoken messages of encouragement that show you value their input. You might say:

'Good point.' 'Good question.' 'Excellent idea!' 'That's really helpful.' 'I think we can all agree with that.' 'You've made a good point, would anyone else like to contribute?'

The Rule of Attention

The general view is that attention starts to slide after 7 to 10 minutes of concerted concentration. Knowing this, the presenter needs to inject something to stimulate the audience and pace the introduction of different techniques to restore engagement. These can be:

- Stopping after ten minutes or so to ask the audience whether they have understood what you've covered so far
- Asking one of your prepared questions to someone in the audience. If you receive a good response to a question, praise the participant ask if anyone has something more to add
- Picking someone in the audience to get their reaction to the event
- Asking an audience member to share an experience related to the subject matter
- Relating the topic of the presentation to something that is currently in the news or of interest beyond the business sector
- Telling a business story – either based on your experience or an anecdote about a well-known personality
- Telling a story about something you got wrong and showing what you learned as a result
- Getting the audience to participate in a task
- Breaking the audience into groups and making each group make a contribution that captures their viewpoint

- If appropriate for the occasion, doing something unexpected. Perhaps streaming a video or playing a piece of music or introducing a surprise guest to the proceedings
- Using a flip chart or white board to make a note of comments or inviting an audience member to come up from the audience and participate. The flip chart can be used after the meeting as key points for further discussion
- Perhaps offering a prize or a reward for some kind of accomplishment in the meeting.

VAK – Visual Auditory and Kinaesthetic – Learning Attributes for Audience Engagement

To engage, involve and perhaps entertain an audience, having an understanding of three learning attributes can be very useful. People are often a combination of these attributes, but essentially this method is an aid to getting a greater understanding of overall personality characteristics. For a presenter this can translate into using different triggers to engage different people. Often you can identify core traits by the type of language people use, as you'll see in the chart below.

The lead characteristics for each type are:
1. Visual: People who learn visually by seeing and reading – their sight is their chosen way of assimilating information
2. Auditory: People who reinforce learning by listening and speaking
3. Kinaesthetic: People who lock in learning by touching, feeling and doing.

V-A-K: Visual – Auditory – Kinaesthetic
Identifying Three Personality Modes of Receiving and Processing Learning

Sense Modes	Thinking	Speaking and Responding	Presentation Approach
Visual (Sight)	Tend to look upwards when thinking. Eyes up to the left when thinking constructively and up to the right when recalling thoughts	To such terms as: I get the picture; I see that now, What's your perspective? What's your view? Can you show me?	Accent on visual communication: charts, images, photos, diagrams to reinforce learning
Auditory (Hearing)	Look straight ahead to the left when thinking constructively and right when recalling from memory	I hear you, That rings a bell, That sounds right, I like the sound of that, Listen to that, Can you tell me, I like what you're saying, Sounds good	Tell business stories, play music or spoken word recordings, play sounds, capture attention and speak directly to them
Kinaesthetic (Touch)	Tend to look downwards when thinking to the left and down to the right when recalling thoughts	How does that grab you? Can you grasp that? How does that feel? I have a good feeling about that. I'd like to try that, I'll give it a go	Involve in activity, role play, standing, 'doing' things, ask to physically participate and demonstrate

Rehearse, Rehearse, Rehearse
80% rehearsing, 20% delivering

Rehearsing is not only about learning original content; rehearsing gives you the opportunity to see if all the elements are working together in harmony. Time spent rehearsing is never wasted. It gives you time to spot anything you've missed, whether anything is incorrect or if you need further research or clarification of source material. A final run-though gives you time to consider whether presentation charts are effective and put last touches to supporting documents and hand-outs. Taking a copy of the presentation material allows you to make your notes and prepare written links between the slides. It is wise to have a copy of the slides close to hand so you know what is coming next, as you always need to be thinking ahead.

If you have a section where you are reading to the audience from a prepared script, make sure you've spoken it out loud beforehand to make sure the words flow. Sometimes words look okay on the page and in your head, but speaking them out loud creates a different dynamic. Often there are too many words that jumble and crash into each other when on the tongue. If you're nervous this only makes matters worse. A tip is to make sure your script is easy to read by putting it in a 14-point font with lines set at 1.5 apart.

Pacing the Presentation

As you rehearse you can get a good idea of the time it will take to cover section by section. If the main content has a three-part structure you need to add time for a general introduction, for questions and a final summary to be factored into your timing plan. If the total time you have is an hour, as a guide it could be charted like this:

Section	Content	Timing Guide Minutes	10-Minute Attention Refresher
1. Introduction	Presentation rules	5	
2. Background	Business opportunity	10	Audience understanding check
3. Main Proposal	Objectives and recommendation	15	Refresher statement when appropriate
4. Implementation	Execution of concept	10	Natural break after this section? Recap of key points
5. Questions	Audience reaction	10	Q&A session – manage as host
6. Summary and Next Steps and Close	Recap of main points Points taken from audience reaction Action points Close	10	Agreed strategy Call to action Timing Plan Arrangement of any further query sessions
Total Time		60 minutes	

What to Wear

What you wear giving a presentation is pretty important. As always in these things it's as much about what you feel is right and what is right for the occasion. Ninety seconds are all it takes for people to make a judgement and figures show that as high as 93% of first impressions are non-verbal as people make decisions based by your body language, the way you hold yourself, the clothes you're wearing and whether you seem to be tense or relaxed.

For men it is easier to choose a suit as the accepted uniform of business. Yet if the suit is crumpled and way out of fashion, if the tie is of another age, if the shirt is not properly ironed, if shoes are scuffed and dirty and if hair is looking unkempt then people immediately start to make negative assumptions. Even if everything else looks good, remember to give your shoes a clean as they may be at eye-level if you're standing on a stage. If you're giving a talk on dress-down Friday or in a casual meeting, unless you are the head of global software company, it is best not to wear jeans and be at the smart end of smart casual.

For women colour, is a delicate choice. Blues and greys register business authority. Lighter greens and blues are fresher and are seen positively. Reds are bright signals that stand out as assertive choices. Whether you are male or female, whatever you choose make sure you feel comfortable and try to avoid wearing something for the first time in case it is too tight, especially collars for the boys, and you don't want to be breaking-in a new pair of shoes and wincing in pain.

SECTION 2

SPEAKING AND PRESENTING SKILLS

5

BUILDING CONFIDENCE AND OVERCOMING SHYNESS

Would you rather walk the plank than speak in front of an audience?

This is not as crazy as it sounds. The very idea of speaking to a group of people and being in the spotlight is to many a fate worse than death. In Chapter 5, I'm handing over to Steve Engwell, who will explain ways to overcome shyness and provide a visualisation exercise you can practise to ease negative feelings and help prepare to speak in a business or public setting.

Steve Engwell – NLP Master Practitioner
"Our beliefs are the stories we tell ourselves. Change the story to change the belief"

What is NLP?

NLP, or Neuro Linguistic Programming, was created by Richard Bandler and John Grinder in California, USA during the 1970s. They studied human excellence and were curious about 'the difference that made the difference' between people who were good at what they did and those who were excellent.

NLP is a model of communication. It focuses on how we individually think about our values and beliefs and how this in turn creates the emotional states, behaviour and identity for our inner world, which then manifests externally. It's about the language of the mind using pictures, sounds, feelings, taste, smell, and self-talk. We are what we think and feel.

Our behaviour has a structure and this can be modelled (that's both our conscious and unconscious patterns), learned (like a strategy being run) and changed (re-programmed). Excellent behaviour can be duplicated. NLP can be described as:

N – Neurology. How our brain and physiology is wired up harmoniously together to allow us to breathe, laugh, walk, eat, learn habits and to feel as we do.

L – Linguistic. The verbal and non-verbal language we use when we talk to ourselves (like stories we tell ourselves) and communicate with other people.

P – Programming. The bringing together and combining of all the above patterns to create our own unique software that we run automatically, just like a computer program to achieve the results we do – good and bad. Put simply, NLP is a set of tools and approaches that modify patterns of thinking that affect the way we behave. Change the way you think and you change the way you feel and act. Doing this will build confidence and help you overcome shyness in every aspect of your life.

Overcoming Shyness or a Lack of Confidence

Did you know that we are born with only two fears – the fear of falling and the fear of loud noises?

These are said to be built into our DNA and have been passed down through the generations as a survival mechanism for 'fight' or 'flight'. Their sole purpose is to keep you alive and create emotion that will motivate you to move away from danger.

Did you know therefore that any other fears that we subsequently exhibit are learned behaviours and they are quite often picked up in our very early formative years? This has often been described as an innate form of learning from situations, circumstances and from typically influential authority figures around you as you grow up, e.g. parents, guardians, teachers, etc.
Did you know that if this behaviour was learned behaviour, then it can be unlearned?

Can you begin to imagine the sense of freedom as you throw off those shackles to tackle what were once **perceived** as your greatest fears and inhibitions and move forward to transform your life? The good news is that this can be achieved with true commitment and determination to change.

For many people the mere thought of stepping out into a group to deliver a presentation, to give a talk or conduct a seminar can bring back familiar feelings of dread, emotional anxiety and a sinking feeling in the pit of their stomach. Unfortunately this situation can then become compounded by unnecessarily negative self-talk which only goes to reinforces the fear. But where did these negative feelings and emotions come from? What events in earlier life created such a powerful trigger, sufficient to paralyse you, sabotage your future and spoil your enjoyment of life?

Are you really going to want to give up your dreams or should you aim to get rid of those pesky annoyances? These old perceptions can sometimes be described as faulty programming in our brains and are likely to remain with us until they are addressed and corrected. As you grow older, why would you bother to listen to that inner, inexperienced voice of the child? You are now a mature adult who has been part of some wonderful life experiences. To change is to face the fear, lock away those **old beliefs** that are no longer the true you, drop that baggage and enjoy life's opportunities.

> "If one advances confidently in the direction of his dreams, and endeavours to live the life he has imagined, he will meet with a success unexpected in common hours."
> Henry David Thoreau (author, poet, philosopher)

It can be difficult to look back and pinpoint when specific fears started or where they emanated from, however, there is likely to have been a situation during the early part of your life that created a misconception at that time, leading to some faulty programming that manifests itself as a 'limiting belief'. Such fears are often quite irrational and make no real sense to justify why you would allow them to rule you during adulthood. It is worth noting that these are indeed 'beliefs' and not 'truths' as they are something you have chosen to acknowledge and believe to be true.

At this point you may already be reflecting on your own perceived inhibitions and it's good that you should bring these to mind now in readiness to let them go forever. It is time to update any faulty programming, clear and reformat the hard drive to reinstall a new, up-to-date operating system that could be the Windows on your new life.

The Conscious and Unconscious Mind

We all have a conscious mind and we also have an unconscious mind. The unconscious mind stores and organises your memories, but its primary job is to protect you at all times and it will always function for the highest possible intent. Although we process some 2 million pieces of information every second, consciously we may only be aware of 7, plus or minus 2 bits of information, which means a number between 5 and 9 (*George A Miller 1956*). Our awareness is highly selective. For example, until I mention it now you may not be aware of the tip of your left ear, the floor beneath your feet or your back pressing against the chair. By directing your attention you will have brought these back into consciousness – they were always there but are now part of those 7 (+ or – 2) pieces of information. As human beings we generalise, distort and delete information all the time to free our attention and make the whole thing more manageable.

These limiting old beliefs are stored as memories in our unconscious minds and it becomes a question of accessing them to change them. There are a number of possible ways to begin to address this issue so that behaviour and habits can be changed and 'unlearned'. The irrational fear or belief that you hold is likely to have served you in a positive way at some time in the past.

Take young, shy Johnny, who at the age of 5 was asked to come to the front of the classroom to read from a book. Johnny blushes, he has not done this before, and walks out to a sea of faces; he turns to the class, which falls silent, lifts the book and proceeds to read aloud, his nerves making him stutter:

Johnny: *"Eeerrrr... Eric had always wwww... wwwwanted a pppp ppppppeeett pet of his own. A cccc... cccccc... aa... ccc... aaaatt cat. Eerrriiicc thought aaa aaas as he... "*

Teacher: *"Thank you, Johnny, that's fine, you can now sit down".*

Phew, what a relief for Johnny, that was over quickly. He thinks ,"I don't have to read any more to the class today. Job done. Thank you unconscious mind!" And yet, in that very moment a limiting belief was created. The mere act of stammering nervously in front of the teacher quickly got Johnny out of the situation. The unconscious mind can now run a process that can be used to 'protect' that child and can run this process at any time, to spare his anxiety, just like a computer programme.

But when Johnny reaches the age of 22 he is asked to give a presentation in his new job to the Board. In this analogy, Johnny needs a new self-image – would others really want to listen to, observe and emulate the actions of a five-year-old? No... that would be ridiculous, wouldn't it?

The issue isn't that you used to be shy and uncomfortable presenting to a group of people, it's that as an adult you have learned so much that you now have something important to say and share that others truly want to hear and learn from, which means you should now grasp every opportunity to relay your thoughts, ideas and experiences for the benefit of others and to move forward with your life and career aspirations. It's time to change that self-image.

Sometimes we think that holding on makes us strong, but when faced with those pesky demons in our minds, it's all about the letting go. The prospect of presenting to a group of people may seem daunting and create an inner turmoil, but this sensation is telling you that this will be a new and worthwhile learning experience.

"The most important psychological discovery of modern times is the discovery of self-image and by learning to modify it and manage it to suit your purposes you gain incredible confidence and power."
Maxwell Maltz (author of Psycho-Cybernetics – 1960)

Home in on What You Want

So let's turn to some basic approaches to begin to update and install new software for the mind, to start to overcome those old habits and beliefs to set you free for a brighter future. It's worth keeping in mind that change can happen quickly in any given situation and that change can be permanent so allow yourself to be surprised when you feel that something has changed and celebrate that.

Our physical brain and nervous system can be likened to a 'servo-mechanism' that is used to operate much like a computer, a mechanical goal-seeking device that strives to achieve a certain goal, like a self-guiding missile seeking out a target, where success or failure depends on the programming.

The mere action of picking up a pen from a table involves a series of automatic and unconscious movements. You are not aware of the series of instructions being issued, relayed and followed between brain, eyes, muscles and limbs – your automatic mechanism is using previously learned and corrected behaviour to form the motion of picking up the pen. *You* own this process and it can be used to perform and achieve more complex tasks. The process remembers successes, forgets failures and the action is repeated as 'habit'. Therefore, if you can pick up a pen, you can speak confidently and persuasively to large audiences.

Well-Formed Outcomes

Goals are important to all of us and without them we will flounder when trying to achieve what we want to in life. The more precisely and positively you can define what you want, the more likely you are to achieve it. It is important to frame what we want in positive terms. We sometimes think of issues in our lives as 'problems', which causes us to get stuck and holds us back.

You can turn a problem into an outcome.

"I don't want to stand up and talk in front of the team."
— *ask, "What would you like instead?"*

"I can't deliver the presentation to a group of complete strangers."
— *ask, "What would happen if you could?"*

Follow a 6-Step Process to Achieve Your Goals

We will now follow a 6-Step process designed to help you programme yourself for success in achieving your goal. This is a comprehensive approach known as achieving a 'Well-Formed Outcome'.

Step 1: State your Aim

So what is the issue, do you truly know where you want to go? Are you going to tackle it or are you going to procrastinate?

"Would you tell me please, which way I ought to go from here?" said Alice.
"That depends a good deal on where you want to get to," said the Cat.

"I don't much care where… " said Alice.
"Then it doesn't matter which way you go," said the Cat.
(Alice in Wonderland, Lewis Carroll)

Alice had no idea and quickly became lost. People tend to put things off and so it is important to actually set a clearly defined goal to focus on.

On a scale of 1 to 10 (1 being low and 10 being high), how much do you want to achieve a goal?

Anything less than 8 and you are likely to fail, so reconsider the goal and make it specific to what you truly want.

Use your creative imagination to identify a goal that is something you passionately want to attain. It should be stated in the positive and must be written down in one punchy sentence and as if you have already achieved it. For example:

"I am a truly confident and accomplished speaker who enjoys delivering regular monthly presentations at the central job club forum."

Goals should be SMART – Specific, Measurable, Achievable and Aspirational (to give some stretch to the challenge), Realistic and Time-Linked.

Writing down your goal will bring clarity, provide motivation and allow you to monitor progress. If you don't write it down it is no more than a wish.

The goal should be shared with someone you trust, admire and respect. This will allow you to be accountable, to be clear, to share and celebrate progress; it yields encouragement, provides support and creates rapport. Research conducted by Dr Gail Matthews (Psychologist at the Dominican University of California) studied procrastination and demonstrated that people who wrote down their goals, shared this information with a friend and sent them weekly updates were on average 33% more successful in accomplishing their stated goals.

Step 2: Evidence

Make sense of your aims. Gaining evidence that you are achieving a goal becomes a motivational force and this can be hard evidence but also *sensory* specific evidence.

We take in our experiences of the world around us from our senses – sight, hearing, touch, smell and taste. We are then able to use our thought processes to recreate those sensory experiences internally. If you remember a pleasant memory you will smile, an unpleasant one will evoke painful emotions and the thought of a favourite food will make us salivate.

The Power of Visualisation

As you close your eyes and focus positively on your written goal it is important to see yourself doing this through your own eyes and to experience the evidence. You can begin to creatively imagine yourself as if you are a confident and competent speaker in front of a large group.

In your head, ask yourself what precisely do you - SEE, HEAR, FEEL, TASTE AND SMELL?

In doing this you are actually making that future state a reality to the unconscious mind. To regularly review and imagine that future adds more detail and reinforces what you want. It may be that you SEE a group of smiling, joyful and intent faces, senior managers nodding approval as they listen to your every word. You SEE yourself standing tall and proud and speaking articulately, delivering powerful points to an interested audience.

You HEAR the upbeat tone of your confident voice, occasional sighs of pleasure and awe from the group, much buzzing interaction and a round of applause at the end. This makes you FEEL strong, exhilarated and excited, as if a pulsating glow is emanating from your chest and rising up through your body. This exercise allows you to begin to mentally visualise or sense that very image where true focus will in turn create internal representations that will manifest as feelings and emotions.

Some people claim they cannot visualise and only see black when closing their eyes. Many wrongly expect to see 3D, vivid images in Technicolor. Yet if you stand and imagine your living room with your eyes closed and do a mental 360 degree turn, you can begin to visualise the placement of the furniture, count the windows, note the type and position of the furniture, paintings, lamps… imagine kneeling down to touch the carpet, note the pattern and texture. If this is difficult then all you have to do is **pretend,** as this becomes real with more practice.

Details of imagery are vitally important in this type of exercise because the unconscious mind cannot distinguish between what is 'imaginary' and what is 'real'.

"Imagination rules the world." – Napoleon Bonaparte

Any thought you repeat over and over, any visual image you create and hold in your mind, over and over, are examples of the 'operating system' that you programme into your unconscious mind. Its job is to store, organise and interpret data from your predominant thoughts. Its job is to attract or help you create the circumstances that match the images and thoughts you have imprinted in it and automate much of your behaviours and thought patterns.

Beliefs are the stories we tell ourselves – change the story, change the belief.

Do you remember?

- In the Disney animation film *Bambi*, Bambi's mother is killed by a hunter halfway through the film
- In the film *Jaws* a decaying head unexpectedly and suddenly pops out of the bottom of the boat in front of scuba divers
- In your dreams that you were falling, trapped, being chased and couldn't breathe?

Did a lump come to your throat with sadness? Did you jump in terror? Was your heart beating faster? Was your adrenaline running? Did you wake up abruptly in a hot sweat?

Absolutely – the unconscious mind took these situations to be reality.

Acting 'as if'

There are no filters in the unconscious levels of the brain to distinguish the difference between imagination and reality and therefore everything is believed to be real. You can therefore use this to your advantage with regular visualisation.

If you can portray or 'act out' the role of something you truly desire and make it look totally believable in your mind, your unconscious mind will take it for reality. Therefore, act *'as if'* and incorporate and portray your conscious goals in your mind consistently and in great detail – and the unconscious will take it for reality.

With practice you will become even better at visualisation and will be able to implant new scenarios in your mind and then make them realistic and compelling. This is rather like making a movie in your mind; you can make this more lively and realistic by using *all your five senses*.

Enhancing Imagery

Any distinctions we can identify with our senses in the external world, we can also make in our internal world. We see colours, sense distances and hear variations in sound in our imagination.

As you imagine being called into your job interview to deliver your presentation, add more vibrant colour to the scene, make it bigger and brighter and bring the imagery more into focus and nearer to you. Have upbeat music playing in your head that grows louder to a great crescendo (why was 'Ride of the Valkyries' played loudly to the airborne troops as they went into battle in the film *Apocalypse Now*?).

This creates a growing excitement, an adrenaline rush culminating in a powerful, all conquering feeling or emotion as you throw open the interview room door and walk boldly in to deliver a profound presentation to a group of complete strangers.

Creating a Habit

Practising mental rehearsals of this kind *regularly* for seven days before an important event will create new neural pathways in the brain and implant the unconscious belief that you will get what you want. Doing this consistently over twenty-one to thirty days will create a new habit.

Just act *'as if'* you are that new person – you can even pretend with conviction. We are what we think and feel – keeping this in mind will give you that special 'boost'.

Mental Rehearsal

These techniques are often used with athletes and sports people. Before a major event they picture the smooth process of achievement playing out on the track, on the pitch or in the pool. A thorough mental rehearsal is conducted **in great detail**, all the way through to a successful end result.

They visualise racing ahead, leading the track, exceeding their personal best and watching that gold medal being placed over their head.

Another important factor to bear in mind – the unconscious mind *does not process negatives.*

"Whatever you do – whatever you do now – do not – do not think of a pink elephant up a tree with dark sunglasses."

What just happened? We think with our imagination therefore always be clear when telling your unconscious mind what to do, think or be; as opposed to telling it what not to do, not to think or not to be. It cannot process negatives and in order to make sense of something it will do that very thing as it does not know the difference.

'Keep it positive' examples:

- *"I am confident in delivering this presentation to the Board."*
- *"I am an interesting person and the whole group will be listening intently to what I have to say."*
- *"I deserve this job as I have a proven track record of experience and have worked hard in preparing for all the assessment processes."*

The word 'cannot' is made up of two words – 'can' and 'not'. As amazing human beings we 'can' do anything, but sometimes we choose 'not' to.

The Law of Attraction

This is the belief that 'like attracts like' and that concentrating on positives or negatives will bring about those positive or negative results using thoughts as pure energy – like a self-fulfilling prophesy. This concept, which dates back to ancient times, has been used more recently by many people, including Brian Tracey, Napoleon Hill and Rhonda Byrne in her book: *The Secret*. But actually, it can be argued that you are doing no more than giving your unconscious mind direction. The unconscious mind is always looking for instructions. It will follow orders and take instructions *literally* and run with them.

Just Do It

The success of this step is of course up to you. You may try to resist doing this if you think you can't be bothered. Some people may say, "Well *I will try* and do this before my interview presentation on Friday." Be very careful of the word 'try' as this presupposes failure. "Oh yes, *I'll try* and come to your party this weekend." You immediately know they will not show. Be forthright, be focused and be positive. You will either attempt this exercise or you will not.

In this extract from *Star Wars Episode V: The Empire Strikes Back*, Yoda is training Luke Skywalker to become a Jedi Knight by asking him to raise the X Wing fighter craft from the lake using the power of his mind':

LUKE: "Oh, no. We'll never get it out now."

Yoda stamps his foot in irritation.
YODA: "So certain are you. Always with you it cannot be done. Hear you nothing that I say?"

Luke looks uncertainly out at the ship.
LUKE: "Master, moving stones around is one thing. This is totally different."

YODA: "No! No different! Only different in your mind. You must unlearn what you have learned."

LUKE: (focusing, quietly) "All right, I'll give it a try."

YODA: "No! Try not. Do. Or do not!! There is no try...."

You already have all the resources you need to be successful.

So what do you choose? To live in fear of public speaking and remain on 'The Dark Side' or use that innate 'Force' within you to strike back and make a success of your life?

You are in charge of your mind and therefore your results. People have all the resources they need to make the changes they want. The internal building blocks that successful people use to create their lives are the same building blocks you possess; it's only a matter of method.

Step 3: Intent

Now it is time to focus your state of mind to direct you towards the goal and to connect you to your beliefs and values. In setting your intent you are connecting your goal with motivation to the future. Intent creates energy and attention towards the future and will cause the unconscious mind to work towards the goal. In Latin 'intent' means to 'stretch, strain or exert' and doing this will create a connection over time with your goal. To set intent is to relay a message to your unconscious mind.

My intention is for you to release your true potential and deliver presentations with confidence and ease. To set the intent for your goal here are some questions for you to consider, then write down your responses.

Why do I want this?
Why is it important to me?
What will I get from getting this?
How will getting this benefit me?

Step 4: Consequence Check

This is sometimes known as a 'Sanity Check' and you should consider whether there are any potential unintended consequences that could occur as a result of you achieving your goal, i.e. is there likely to be a secondary gain from achieving the outcome that you were unaware of? Could this be something negative that you had not foreseen and if so how can that be addressed. Is there likely to be something that you would need to give up? In some cases this step has caused people to reconsider and modify their goal.

For this step you simply need to think *as if* you are in the future. Consider the following and again note your responses.

What are the wider consequences of my action?
What will I lose if I make this change?
What extra will I have to do?
Is it worth it?
How will getting it benefit me?
What will I gain if I make this change?
What is the price of making this change and am I willing to pay it?
What are the good aspects of my present state?
How can I keep those good aspects while making the change that I want?
How will my change affect others, or other aspects of my life?
Does it go against any of their values?
Does this matter?
How will they react?
Do you want the change in any other situation?

Step 5: Action Plan

Now to address the 'how', and again here are questions to consider:
What are the key sequential steps to be taken to achieve the goal?
What are the associated timescales?
Can some tasks be broken down into smaller and more manageable incremental steps?

What resources are needed?

Who do I need help from?

How and when do I get that help?

Is my plan in the form of a list, a table or a mind map?

How do I share the plan with my respected co-conspirator for friendly criticism and feedback?

How do I intend to *celebrate* as I achieve success along the way? Yes, it's ok to celebrate your successes with any milestones – you've earned it, you deserve it.

Step 6: Implement the Plan

The last step is the first step forward to make it happen. Now that you realise that your future is in your hands and within your power to change, shed limiting beliefs and consign negative thinking and actions and insecurities to the past.

Move forward today and consider:

When and how do I start?

What will I do first?

What am I going to do today? This week? This month?

A Final Thought

By following this process carefully you can not only address issues to improve self-confidence for public speaking, but indeed any aspect of your life where you are looking to make a positive change. Maintain a positive and confident self-image always. Remember to always focus on what you want – not what you don't want.

> *"When defeat comes, accept it as a signal that your plans are not sound, rebuild those plans, and set sail once more toward your coveted goal."*
> *Napoleon Hill, Think and Grow Rich.*

6

REDUCING STRESS

Stress before Nerves

Steve Engwell has opened your mind to recognising and overcoming limiting beliefs. The NLP process he outlined can progressively alter the way you think and dramatically change your attitude toward future achievements. A successful future is waiting for you and you will reap the benefits.

In the meantime, while these changes are taking place we all get stressed. There's stress caused by personal or family issues and work-related stress. Ruth Fogg of Stressworx has coined the phrase *'What the mind suppresses the body expresses'.* If you're feeling the effects of stress, whatever the cause, your health suffers; headaches, insomnia, depression and panic attacks are all signposts of stress. If your health is affected your performance in the workplace is affected. On top of the day-to-day anxiety or pressure, if you're asked to speak the red light of panic will start to flash.

It is totally natural to have nerves before you present. These nerves are related to the act of performing and can be managed in ways you will soon learn. Would it not be good if you **only** had those nerves to contend with and were not stressed about a million other things at the same time?

Combating Stress

Here are a few ways to reduce stress levels in your life. Some are designed to blend into your normal pattern of living for long-term benefit. The first set of life-long options delivers the greatest benefit if practised regularly; the length of time you devote to them is flexible depending on how you feel and the time you can reasonably dedicate in your busy life. Even ten minutes in the morning and ten minutes in the evening would open and close your day with calmness.

Life-long Ways to Reduce Stress

1. **Tell your brain to look after your body**

   This is about listening to your body when your brain is physically or mentally pushing too hard. You need to be in-tune with your limits and be mindful not to overstretch your capacity. Take breaks. Breathe fresh air. If possible avoid taking that extra unnecessary journey. Eat and sleep well. Laugh and make time for all the pleasures of life. Listen to music. Treasure your natural physical gifts, don't squander them. You brain will thank you for this by being rested and smarter the next time you use it.

2. **Be alert to signals of stress**

   Being short-tempered, irritable, snappy, having slowed reactions, sensitivity to bright lights or loud noises, wanting to be alone, being uncommunicative, having slouched shoulders, keeping your eyes down, these are all tell-tale signals of stress. You'll know the ones that signal that you're under stress. Recognise and receive these signals, decode the stress messages and act on them.

3. **Make 'quality time' for yourself**

   Get a massage. Go to the gym. Have your hair done. Book a holiday. Walk the dog. Learn to draw. Do something that is purely for you to act as a diversion from pressure. If you like, these activities are de-compression valves of stress. You start stressed, you'll finish feeling human.

4. Meditate

Meditation not only helps you get both your head and body in harmony, it helps you relax, think clearly, improve concentration and sharpen decision making. It also dissipates stress. It does this by combating negative thinking. There are a number of different forms of meditation, some are linked to spiritual traditions but others are purely techniques for relaxation. The ones based on religious teachings usually involve reciting a mantra. Concentrating on the mantra to the exclusion of all else has the effect of cutting through the buzz or white static of interference that surrounds our thoughts. It acts like a sonic passcode to open the door to the inner you.

Two Mantra-Free Meditation Techniques

I. **Let the Listening Run Out** – A superb technique for improving concentration, especially if you work in an open-plan office where interruptions are constant. Ideally you need to be alone in a quiet space. You're about to learn the benefits of zonal listening.

Let's assume you're at home, in a room on your own, sitting on an upright chair, feet without shoes flat on the floor, palms resting gently on your thighs, eyes closed.

First: identify and concentrate on a sound in the **immediate vicinity**. It could be the sound of something within the house or neighbours talking or rain on the windowpane. Focus *only* on that close-by sound for a few moments.

Second: switch your listening to the **middle distance.** This could be traffic in a nearby road, music playing or a dog barking in the middle distance. Concentrate *only* on the sounds of the middle distance.

Third: direct your listening to the furthest sound zone – **the far distance.** This could be a plane flying overhead, the sound of a football match caught in the wind, the mournful cry of a train in the distance. Focus *only* on the sounds of the far distance.

The Result
By practising this technique you'll find that by the time you get to listening zone three – the far distance – your ears will be picking up sounds there but be almost oblivious to sounds in the immediate and middle distance. It's as if your ears have become radar discs sweeping the sky for sound. Your hearing will have crossed different listening zones.

Learning this discipline has the benefit of making you able to 'filter out' sound that you don't want to hear and concentrate only on what you want to listen to. Once again, with practise you will be able to have a conversation with someone face-to-face, in a social situation for example, and be able to tune into people talking at a nearby table and hear what they're saying.

The business benefit is that by learning how to 'zone' your concentration you can minimise interruptions to your thinking and reduce noise to a low background buzz.

2. Body Talk
Body talk is similar to zonal listening but the focus is upon different parts of your body. As with zonal listening, the stress-reducing power of this technique comes from taking your mind away from the things or situations that are causing stress and shifting your mental energy in a totally different direction.

Adopt the same comfortable position, sitting straight on a chair with feet flat on the ground.

Wiggle your toes. Think only of your toes. Then switch your mind to the balls of your feet, then to your ankles. Pause there a moment and connect all your energy thoughts to your feet and ankles. Next slowly work your mental way, eyes tight closed, up to your calves, then stop and consider the feeling of your calf muscles tensing and relaxing, tensing and relaxing. Thighs next, then pelvis, then stomach, chest, arms, elbows, hands, fingers, shoulders, neck, face, then finally to the top of your head, with all the strength of mental concentration flowing up your body.

The Result
In time, when you do this, you will feel the flow of electrical energy touching each part of your body as the wave gently flows from foot to head. Again, the act of directed concentration discards all negative stress energies, making you feel relaxed and refreshed. Plus, perhaps for the very first time you will get to feel what your elbows are doing!

Tapping and EFT – Emotional Freedom Technique

Tapping can quickly reduce stress levels at times of heightened anxiety as it combines both a physical and mental element. Gently tapping with your fingertips on the meridian energy pathway points in your upper body is like applying acupuncture without the needles. The effect is to release negative energies, almost like letting pressured air escape from a car tyre. Using four fingers on either your left or right hand, tap a rhythm on a meridian point at the same time as you say, either out loud or in your head, things or emotions you want to let go and dispel from your body. The act of tapping restores and balances your energies. It's almost as if you are mentally and physically rebooting your body. Tapping is a method of calming yourself before you speak. I can personally vouch for its effectiveness. To begin you set the intention of releasing stress and replacing the negative effect with positive energy. You can start tapping in this sequence using either your left or right hand. You may feel a tingling sensation as the meridian points are tapped as if the static is being released.

1. Tap on the 'Karate' chop point on the side of your hand
2. Tap up your neck to the top of your head
3. Tap in the centre of you eyebrows
4. Tap with both hands at the side of your eyes
5. Tap below your nose
6. Tap on the centre point of your chin
7. Tap your collarbone
8. Tap the top centre points of your chest – the sore spots on the diagram
9. Tap on your torso under your arm
10. Tap on the inside of your wrists, near your pulse points
11. Tap gently on the top of your hands behind your knuckles
12. Tap on the side of your hand in the karate chop position in the diagram

As you tap say words of affirmation to encourage stress release. You may say:

"I'm going to stop thinking negative thoughts."
"I'm going to think and act positively."
"I'm going to de-stress my body."
"I'm going to feel calm and relaxed."
"Today, I'm going to speak slowly, clearly and be in control."
"I'm going to shed nerves and be the best I can be."
"I'm going to make myself proud."
"I'm going to be confident."

Before and after tapping, breathe deeply to expand your chest and release the 'old' air of negativity out. In the moments after you finish tapping you may feel completely balanced and ready again to surge forward.

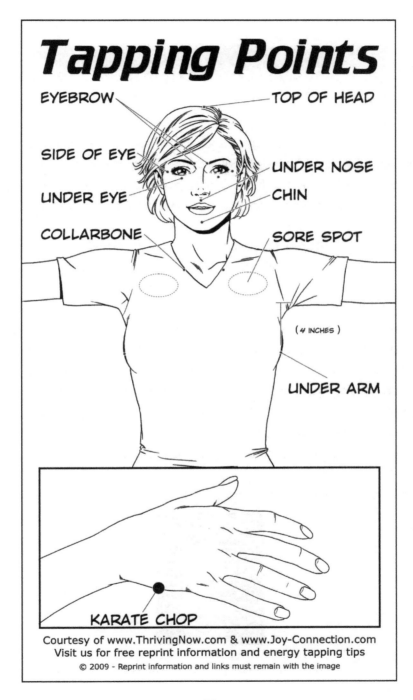

Tapping Points

EYEBROW

TOP OF HEAD

SIDE OF EYE

UNDER NOSE

UNDER EYE

CHIN

COLLARBONE

SORE SPOT

(4 INCHES)

UNDER ARM

KARATE CHOP

Courtesy of www.ThrivingNow.com & www.Joy-Connection.com
Visit us for free reprint information and energy tapping tips
© 2009 - Reprint information and links must remain with the image

7

MANAGING NERVES

What have Stephen Fry, John Simm, Robbie Williams, Hugh Grant, Salma Hayek, Judy Dench, Barbara Streisand and Sir Laurence Olivier have in common? At one time or another they've all suffered from stage fright. So you're not alone if you get a little nervous before stepping into the spotlight. You're in good company.

"The only thing we have to fear is fear itself."
Franklin Delano Roosevelt – in his first USA
Presidential Inaugural Address in 1933

When it comes to speaking there are two fear factors at play: the private feelings and the career and business pressures. The personal ones relate to how we feel about our own abilities and our worries about our own performance. Will I dry up, lose my thread, forget my lines or embarrass myself in some way? The business pressures could add a further layer of concern if the presentation is in front of senior people or the subject matter is of vital importance to the company, or if you are asked to present to a large group of people for the first time.

That's it then. Overcome fear and we'll be alright. But how?

Sally Hindmarch, Managing Director of Partners with You

Having reached Chapter 7 you know how to prepare fully. You know how to pitch to an audience and you know how to prepare a presentation script, you know your subject inside out and you've rehearsed exhaustively. That's half the battle. The second half is learning from Steve's NLP advice and you're about to receive some highly practical advice from Sally Hindmarch of Partners with You.

Partners with You use the skills of professional actors, skills they learned in drama school and have developed during their film, theatre and television experience to overcome nerves, mentally prepare themselves, project their voice and use their gestures and body language, to maximum effect. Sally is about to share some insights and exercises with you. Some of the exercises are ones that you will immediately feel the benefit of. Others are ones that you need to practise to become more proficient at them.

A Secret of Successful Presenting:
Get into Character – Change into the more confident 'You'

The masks of Janus are a traditional symbol of the theatre. Actors in Greek theatre were able to play different roles within a play by simply changing the mask they wore and then projecting different personalities, different characters with their body actions. The significant connection with Partners with You is that actors 'get into character' before taking the stage. You can do this too. When you present, you perform.

The key moment is the transition from your everyday self, your self-image, your own perception of yourself that may be shy or introverted, into the more extrovert you. It is the confident side of you that you project to the audience. How many times have you witnessed famous actors come alive on stage or on screen who then slip back into their real selves as quiet and very private individuals when the curtain comes down? As actors they return to their personal default positions. Psychologically you step into the performer in you, a performer who is not hampered with limiting beliefs and who is there to give the gift of the messenger to the audience.

You may have butterflies the size of bats in your tummy but the person you will project to the audience is the confident 'you' who is calm and in control. By overcoming nerves, you will be able to deliver your message effectively.

And breathe…

Breathing deeply for a few minutes helps to reduce stress and quieten nerves before your speak. The actions of breathing deeply in a controlled, even rhythm send signals to the brain that in turn help the body to release tension and lessen anxiety. Breathing inwards fills the lungs with oxygen that stimulates the brain. Exhaling rids the body of spent air containing carbon dioxide and other gases. The fresh oxygen brings waves of fresh energy to your system.

Practise this regular routine.

1. Sit up or stand up straight and exhale, breathing out through your mouth, pursing your lips and blowing out until you feel there is no more air in your lungs.
2. Breathe in slowly through your nose, feel your chest and rib cage expand.
3. Keep breathing inwards until your chest feels stretched.
4. Hold the breath for a moment then breathe out through your mouth.

Repeat the exercise for a few minutes, concentrating on the act of breathing, eyes closed and relaxing your face and feel the tension ease from your shoulders.

Exercises to Ease Tension

With practice, you can bring back the memory of being relaxed to actually make you feel relaxed again. When you're relaxed your voice will feel and sound easier. Here are two exercises, one to relax your neck and throat and one to ease tension from your shoulders. The physical workout will stretch and exercise muscles to ease tightness.

Neck and Throat

1. Sitting or standing, drop your head forward, pull up slowly and feel the muscles in the back of your neck pulling it up.
2. Drop your head to one side, stretch it slightly then pull up straight.
3. Repeat this on the other side, feel the muscle stretch then slowly pull your head up straight again.
4. Drop you head forward and roll it from side to side then bring it up to the centre position.
5. Tense your shoulder muscles feel the tension then release it – feel the difference.
6. Lift your chin up, stretch and hold to feel the tension on your upwardly extended throat – release and feel the difference as the muscles relax.
7. Nod your head gently forward and back; it should feel poised not tense.
8. Roll your head on your shoulders in a circular motion, first one way then the other.

Shoulder Relaxation

1. Lift your shoulders up gently then drop them.
2. Drop them even further – you usually can.
3. Repeat 2 or 3 times
4. Roll your shoulders in small circles from front to back.

5. Then back to front
6. Repeat 2 or 3 times
7. Let your shoulder sit for a moment and remember the feeling of ease.

Managing Nerves by Creating a Comfort Zone in Your Mind

Sally gives this advice to create a comfort zone of confidence in your head.

> *"Create some affirmations around something you are good at and use them often. Anything that extends your comfort zone will build your confidence. Look at other things you can do or success you've achieved that will make you feel good about yourself."*

On the same subject, Steve Engwell has a practical NLP method of creating a Circle of Confidence.

> *"One of the methods you can use to summon up your confidence in a crisis is a mental technique from NLP (Neuro Linguistic Programming) called the 'Circle of Confidence'. The technique gives you the ability to summon up the memory and relive the warm sense of satisfaction of that achievement. In effect you are about to create a memory 'anchor' to recall whenever you need it to ease pressure and build confidence."*

Here are some steps for creating and using a mental Circle of Confidence that you need to practise ahead of time in order to be able to draw upon it at will.

6 Steps to Create a Circle of Confidence

1. In advance of speaking to an audience or making a presentation, close your eyes and imagine an invisible circle on the floor, perhaps like a circle created by a spotlight beam. Make it about 3 feet in diameter and 2 feet in front of you, something large enough for you to mentally walk into and be bathed in the light. You are on your own without any distractions.

2. Recall a time when you were wonderful at what you were doing. Remember exactly when that was, pinpoint the date, the month, the day and the time. *Put yourself back in that memory and see it through your own eyes.*

   Imagine that everything is going brilliantly and you are bright, funny, happy, confident, full of energy and a great success. You are balanced, creative and powerful, together with any other positive states that come to mind. You want all those positive emotions to come up and flood your body with the good feelings and emotions of that time as you delivered a confident performance and exhibited feelings of excellence.

3. Focus on those states and step forward into the circle, into that person that you were then – and are now.
   You may notice that closing your eyes will simply *intensify* the moment as you focus even more… that's right:

   SEE what you see – perhaps a sea of smiling faces, looks of admiration, looks of great interest and intensity

   HEAR what the sounds are that surround you – the sound of your confident voice speaking slowly and clearly and people listening with rapt attention

   FEEL what you feel – importantly, how does all this now make you feel… a sense of glowing pride inside, a soft but warm sensation on your back as if there may be a divine presence behind you that is willing you to do well… and you know you can, can't you?

Then STEP out of the circle having totally captured the memory experience. To seal the moment, briefly think about something else. This 'breaks state', i.e. simply interrupts the current state before moving into a different one.

4. To test the memory anchor you have just created step back into that circle and see what happens. Step out. Does that feeling of well-being and confidence flood back?

5. When you stepped into the circle, did you notice how you will be different in future in the way that you behave and be better prepared?

6. Mentally pick up the circle and take it with you to throw down to the floor and use again and again whenever you need it to give you a boost.

Nerves are Natural – so be Natural

Anyone who says they don't get nervous is probably saying it as a kind of internal conversation to deny the fact that they are nervous. If you're tense, it's to be expected. Try not to over-think the situation and make it into a monster. You may think that you're entering a lion's den but in reality most people, your colleagues, your workmates, want you to succeed. Why? Because they would be nervous if they had to do what you are about to do and are relieved that they're not having to do it.

Consider this.

1. You don't have to be perfect. Don't set the bar high in your own mind. You are not a professional television presenter. Be realistic.

Don't beat yourself up. You will get better the more practise you get. Even the greatest orators and presenters started somewhere.

2. Everyone makes mistakes. The thing is to accept them, rectify them quickly if you can, if you can't, apologise and move on. Get things in proportion.

3. Visualise a positive outcome. Imagine smiling faces, people clapping, words of congratulation, words of encouragement.

4. Remember that you've worked hard on the preparation and are well versed in your subject. If someone asks a question you can't immediately answer, compliment them on asking it and praise them for making a worthwhile contribution to the discussion. This deflects any negativity from the fact you don't have an answer. As mentioned before, say that you will have an answer for them shortly or you may even ask anyone else in the room to become involved and shed light on the matter. No one will expect you to know everything about everything. Be natural, be normal and sort it out without allowing one question to derail the flow of the presentation.

5. Don't overcomplicate your presentation aids. Keep them simple and easy to physically control.

6. Don't use your presentation as an opportunity to try something new. Until you have built your confidence, remain in a comfort zone of known elements. For example, if you're not familiar with using a particular piece of equipment don't use it. If you're tempted to break people into groups, practise it before you introduce it.

Nourish Your Nerves – Eating and Drinking Tips before You Perform

When it comes to the time to speak, the last thing you want is for something you've done before or during the presentation to spoil your performance. You've got to feel confident in your own skin. Feeling right helps calm nerves and helps you concentrate. Let's focus on breakfast, lunch and liquids.

At breakfast, before a morning presentation, keep it light with cereals and fruit. Try to limit the intake of dairy products as dairy can cause the build-up of mucous on the vocal chords, causing you to cough to clear the cloying sensation. If you're hungry mid-morning have a snack as you will need something in your stomach to avoid it making growling noises. I've found that a banana eases hunger and gives you an energy boost too.

At lunch, don't eat a heavy meal that takes time for the body to digest; allow at least an hour or two before presenting. Heavy meals make you sluggish. Avoid rich and spicy food, strong flavours and garlic (in case you're breathing over the CEO!). Avoid alcohol – until the celebrations afterwards.

Drinks-wise, limit or avoid diuretics like tea and coffee, which can dry out the vocal chords to make any dry-mouth feeling caused by nerves to get even worse. Don't take energy drinks with high a caffeine content or carbonated fizzy drinks as they could alter your mood.

Hydrate with water before you start and have a bottle of water on-hand during your speech. Turning and taking a sip of water during the meeting allows you valuable moments to gather your thoughts and to mentally take a break for a few seconds to think of an answer or a question. However, be careful drinking chilled water as very cold liquid causes the throat and vocal chords to contract.

In summary:
Yes to:
Water and light foods, little tea and careful with the coffee!
No to:
Heavy, spicy foods and eating anything new you haven't eaten before – no risks please. And avoid alcohol.

Right, you've prepared, you've shed the stress, you've managed the nerves, you've hydrated and you're ready to do some exercises and learn some techniques to make you perform like a pro.

8

SPEAKING SKILLS EXERCISES
AND TECHNIQUES

Research has underlined the power and importance of the first impression. It revealed that the initial impact is determined by body language: the posture you adopt, the gestures you use and the eye contact you make before you say anything at all. When you do speak, impressions are shaped by your tone of voice and how you sound. Sometimes it's not what you say, but how you and your body say it.

Annie Farr, Professional Actor
Principal member of Sally's coaching team

Annie hales from Northern Ireland and has been a professional actress since 1991, working extensively in theatre, TV, film and radio. Theatre credits include *The Playboy of the Western World* and *Peer Gynt* at the National Theatre. Her TV and film work includes *Never Better, Bonekickers* for the BBC and *The Worst Week of My Life, Silent Witness* and *Dream On.* Annie is one of the founding workshop leaders at Partners with You and heads their script-writing and workshop development team.

The content for this chapter has been written following an interview with Annie and with the benefit of my attending the Partners with You 'Presentation and Confidence-Building Workshop'.

1. Body Language

We don't just receive messages through the words that are used. We are constantly 'reading' how they are delivered; through the tone of voice (the way that they are said) and visually (through body language). When preparing to speak, most people concentrate on the words that they are going to say and spend very little time on the way that they are going to say them. We would argue that you will never speak well if you haven't thought about how you will say your piece.

Feeling confident, being confident and showing you're confident are all about the type of image you project through words and actions. They start from the first handshake. The first time you make physical contact with someone triggers signals that instantly form powerful impressions. A limp handshake implies a weak personality or can be perceived as dismissive or disengaged. At the other end of the spectrum, a crushing grip can give the impression of aggression or over-confidence.

Decode the Handshake Style	Impression Created
Limp	Anxious, low self-esteem, unsure, ineffective, dismissive, disengaged
Forceful, tight grip	Arrogant, overpowering, too assertive
Firm	Confident, in control, to be trusted
2 hands together, 1 over the other	Danger of seeming insincere or trying too hard
2nd hand – over forearm	Controlling
2nd hand – under forearm	Supportive but can be misread as patronising
2nd hand – on shoulder	We are going to be friends

What your body is saying speaks before you do. Similarly, what others are saying with their body language or gestures can be indicative of their state of mind or attitude. Here are some ways to translate this unspoken language. You cannot rely on each of these meanings if taken individually, but if you see several of these gestures continuing as you watch them, you'll get a fair indication of what they're feeling.

Reading Gestures

Gesture	Can indicate
Stroking or twisting hair	Anxiety
Ear touching	A need for comfort
Body hugging	A need for reassurance
Face touching	Anxiety about letting words out or a need to mask what's being said
Jewellery fiddling	Nerves, distress or worry
Finger tapping	Impatience

Exercises for a Confident Posture

There is a correlation between your message and your posture so it is important that you stand or sit with confidence or, as we would say, positively. This means that your audience will consider what you are saying without being distracted by the way you look.

Become Taller and More Commanding

Stooped shoulders or dropping your head forward transmits a lack of confidence. Just standing straighter with your shoulders back and head straight transforms the impression, lengthens the body and means that you gain height. You will immediately feel better.

'The String' is one exercise to achieve this.

- Imagine there's a single piece of string running right through your body from foot to head. The string comes up from the floor, runs right through your body and leaves from the middle of your skull, as if you are a puppet on a string.
- In your mind, pull the string straight to pull yourself upright and raise your height (we've seen people increase their height by at least an inch by pulling their string!).
- Standing like this prevents you from collapsing in the core, which would mean that the diaphragm couldn't engage and you wouldn't be able to take a 'proper' breath. This in turn would affect your concentration, muscle tension and mean you are more likely to run out of breath when speaking. 'Spiro' is the Latin word for breath; 'inspiration' comes from this word.

'The Bolero' improves your posture and opens the rib cage to help deeper breathing.

- Imagine you're wearing a Spanish-style bolero jacket.
- In your mind, imagine that someone comes behind you and gently pulls down at the centre of the bottom of the jacket.
- Your shoulders will pull back slightly (you don't want to look like a pigeon), this will allow your chest to expand so you can fill your lungs to take the stage.

Using the string and the bolero will mean you will look more confident as well as helping you to feel more confident and able to take to the stage.

Sitting Pretty – Sitting Positively

Normally, you'll be sitting waiting for the presentation to begin. You can use this preparation time by mindfully running through this exercise.

- Push your bottom into the back of the chair.
- Sit upright with your shoulders pulled back and square.
- Pull your head up so you have a level gaze.

- Allow your legs to be relaxed with your feet flat on the floor.
- Place your hands palms-down on your thighs.
- As you sit quietly and alert, concentrate on your breathing, drawing deeply then exhaling to bring fresh oxygen into your body.

Body Awareness

As you've been pulling the string, wearing the bolero jacket and sitting pretty you've been thinking and focusing on your body. Body awareness builds on those exercises by asking what you look like to yourself and to others and what impression you give. Once you've completed these two exercises you will spot what you like and what needs work.

Freeze Frame

- In the privacy of your own room, suddenly stop and freeze as if you're playing a game of statues.
- Look at your body from someone else's perspective. What impression do you give? Are you happy with that frozen image?
- Be honest, how would you like to be seen?
- What would you change?

Mirror Image

1. Sit or stand in front of a long mirror.
2. Look at yourself from head to foot and see what image you are portraying when you are 'natural'.
3. Then strike a number of different poses and see how you alter the impressions you make. Each time you strike a new pose, look at your:
   - Stance: are you slouched or upright, are you looking down at the floor or on the level?
   - Shoulders: are they rounded or tight?
   - Arms: are your arms folded or held at your side?

- Hands: are your hands clasped together or by your side?
- Feet: do your toes point inwards, do you rock on your feet, do you stand with your feet together or apart, do you look at your shoes?

Bearing in mind what you've learned from other exercises, practise sitting, standing and walking positively. Pull yourself up to your full height, chin level, shoulders back, feeling light on your feet and move smoothly around the floor. Burn these images into your mind to see how more aware and confident you seem, with a new positivity while still being natural. Switching to the positive 'presentation' you from the 'off-stage' you will, in time, become second nature.

Reflections of You

You can use your mirror to send you a message. On top of the visual feedback, the mirror reflects the way you look and sound. This is an aid to help you control emotional leakage from your body. Leakage occurs when you're unsure of yourself, when your whole demeanour could be projecting nervous uncertainty. This exercise helps you identify and rectify the situation.

1. Stand in front of a mirror and talk to the mirror, say something, anything.
2. Look at the way you're coming across.
3. Focus on the way your voice sounds.
4. As you speak, are you looking assertive?
5. Are you standing positively?
6. As you look and sound more effective you will be. Speak slower than your normal delivery rate, concentrate on the clarity of your voice.
7. The mirror will play back a more confident person. Notice how you feel as you realise how confident you look. Capture that assured image and your feelings in your head. Burn it into your mind so you can reproduce and replay this positive image at will.

2. Vocal Warm Ups

Before you take to the sports field, before you start jogging, before you lift weights in the gym you have to warm up. Before you present, you have to warm up your voice. Unless you limber up your vocal chords, stretch them, make them hum, wake them up, there is a great danger of your voice cracking, drying up and making you cough right in the middle of your pitch. When you present you ask more of your voice. It will be pressed into action for a sustained length of time. Respecting your voice means to think of it as your musical instrument. Do not dehydrate it by drinking tea or coffee. Keep it moist and drink water beforehand and during the session.

Warming up your shoulders, neck and facial muscles will ease tension and tightness in the body. Here are some exercises to start the warm up.

Engage your Body

These exercises gently pass the message to your body that it's time to go to work.

1. Stand straight, lift and tighten your shoulder-blade muscles, release and let your shoulders drop; repeat this two or three times.
2. Pant gently, feel the outward release of air tighten you stomach muscles; think about the effect.
3. Lower your chin, stretching your neck forward, then slowly roll your

head from side to side three times, stop at the forward point and pull your head up slowly counting to five. Feel your neck muscles respond and stretch from these neck rolls.

Mouth and Jaw Exercises

The more flexible and 'open' your mouth and jaw, the richer the vocal resonance. This also helps with clarity and diction.

The Mouse that Roared

1. Stand in front of a mirror and open your mouth as wide as it will go, feeling your cheeks, mouth and lips really stretch, like the roar of a wild animal.
2. Hold the stretch for a second then close your mouth down tight, purse your lips and close down your facial muscles to a meek little mouse.
3. Repeat the exercise and feel the elasticity coming back into your facial muscles.

The Big Chew

1. Drop your jaw gently and open and close your mouth.
2. Imagine that you are chewing in great circles like a cow chewing the cud.
3. Place your hands just under your ears at your jaw joints and massage with your fingertips as you open and close your mouth. Be very gentle – this is a delicate joint so don't push too hard.
4. Draw the jaw down with your fingers and feel the heaviness.
5. Yawn so your jaw and throat are wide open.

3. Voice Resonance– Good Vibrations

Resonance is the vibration of the voice. It produces a richer, warmer sound that gives your voice weight and depth. Resonance comes from vibrations within the chest, the mouth and behind the larynx, at the top of the head and in the nasal passages and sinuses.

Feel those Vibrations

1. Start to hum in the chest; start low and steadily hum higher.
2. Place your hand on your chest and feel the vibrations.
3. Feel the vibrations by placing your hand on the back of your neck, face and the top of your head.
4. Continue humming at a comfortable level.
5. As you hum, tap your chest vigorously.
6. Change the sound of your humming from a 'MMMM' sound to an 'AH' sound. Feel the intensity of the vibrations as they resonate through your rib cage.

4. Pitch and Inflection

Pitch is the range of notes in the sound you create. It is the difference between singing in a monotone or producing a more interesting and varied sound. Differences in pitch are achieved by differences in the length and thickness of the vocal chords. For higher notes the vocal chords are thinner and shorter; lower notes are produced when the vocal chords are longer and thicker. Typically, when women become nervous their voices become shrill, while men's voices tend to drop lower. When you're nervous the voice tends to lose its natural rhythm. These exercises will help to make your voice more flexible and give you control of the sound you make.

High/Low Humming

Humming just before a presentation reinforces your vocal warm-up and helps you hit and maintain an even pitch.

1. Start by humming at a comfortable, normal pitch.
2. Lower the pitch until you are humming as low as you can (ladies, remember this pitch point).
3. Raise the pitch of your voice back to your comfortable level.
4. Then raise your pitch as high as you can (men, remember this pitch point).
5. Repeat the exercise but push yourself to go even higher and lower.
6. Finish by returning to your normal humming pitch.

5. Placing Your Voice Forward

Looking after your voice, easing pressure on your voice is a key element of presenting confidently. The effect of a tight or constricted voice can quickly become apparent. One minute you are doing fine, the next the voice is cramping as the vocal chords lose moisture. The solution is to project sound forward from your throat into your mouth around your teeth and lips. Placing is the art of 'putting' your voice in front of your face and away from your throat. A throat voice is deep and sombre, a voice placed forward is brighter and more alive. This exercise will help project your voice forward.

1. Relax your shoulders and neck.
2. Take a deep breath, count to 3 and start to hum.
3. Move your hum to an OOO to create a MMM MOO sound as you purse your lips.
4. Repeat 3 times
5. Change to MMM MAAH
6. Repeat 3 times
7. Change to MMM MEE
8. Repeat 3 times
9. Change to MMMMM – Many Maids Milking on a May Morning
10. Repeat 3 times

6. Diction and Clarity

When adrenalin is pumping, you speak faster and words can get jumbled and indistinct. The faster you speak the harder it is for your audience to keep up. Diction and clarity are controlled by your lips and tongue. By working these muscles you make them and you more fluent. Take it gently and work them like this:

Tongue
1. Stick your tongue out.
2. Move your tongue from side to side.
3. Imagine you're cleaning the outside of your teeth with your tongue.
4. Switch and clean the inside of your teeth with your tongue.
5. Try to touch the tip of your nose with your tongue.
6. Stroke the tip of your mouth with your tongue.
7. Curl your tongue into a pipe shape.
8. Sing out La La La La with your tongue flipping up and down.
9. Repeat this as often as you like.

Lips
1. Smile a big wide smile.
2. Move your mouth slowly from a smile to making an OOO sound.
3. Speed it up.
4. Move your mouth from a little OOO to a big OOO.
5. Do an impression of a big fat fish kiss.
6. Move your mouth from side to side.
7. Chew your lips (not with your teeth! – just gums).
8. Blow raspberries to relax your lips.
9. Work your lips in a gentle circular motion with your fingertips to relax them fully – feel them tingle.
10. Repeat the above.

Use tongue twisters to loosen your facial muscles and warm up your mouth, lips and tongue just before your presentation.

Tongue Twisters

1. Red Lorry , Yellow Lorry
2. Red Leather Yo-Yo, Yellow Leather Yo-Yo
3. Peemly Paimly Larly Looly
4. Bibbidy Bobbidy Bought a Bat
5. Ken Dodd's Dad's Dog's Dead

Chapter Round Up

There is no reason, no reason at all, why you cannot use this advice to boost your confidence and presentation presence. Until this point you may have been more concerned with the creation of a presentation rather than giving it. By taking these tips you can improve your performance considerably. Partners with You runs regular personal training sessions with small groups. Recently I was invited by Sally to attend. I remember one person at the start of the day who was so nervous and self-conscious that she could hardly speak above a whisper. By the end of the day she had shed so much negative baggage she was flying high with confidence, her self-esteem had rocketed.

You too can let your body language talk for you . You can remember the breathing exercises, voice drills and exercises to conquer fear and put on a fine performance.

9

PRESENTING ONLINE

It's only a matter of time before you will be asked to present online. The versatility of online presenting is a favoured communication tool for every size of business worldwide. Whatever time zone you live in, whatever type of business you run, whatever use you make of it, education, sales or consultancy, online presentation is one communication medium it will pay you to become fluent in. But, as with any communication medium, you need to know how best to use it and integrate it within your overall communcation strategy.

1. Presenting Webinars

This is a blog I wrote after my first experience as a guest presenter delivering a webinar.

Webinar Presentations – 12 Tips for First Timers

If you're reading this the chances are your boss has asked you to give your first webinar presentation. Either that or you've witnessed the rapid growth of webinars and want to grasp this fantastic opportunity to put your message across. Either way, it's a presentation format with its own challenges and rewards. Mastering the challenges will produce an attractive and effective communication tool with massive possibilities.

Remember, as with many things, practise makes perfect, so don't beat yourself up if at first it goes badly wrong – as it did for me.

The weirdness started when I picked up the mic and started talking to myself without human feedback. It's really strange when you're used to having people to react with, when you can see straight away if they understand what you're saying. Doing a conventional presentation allows you to gauge the right pace, the right speed of delivery (not too fast, not too slow) and to check whether people are keeping up by watching the looks on their faces. In a webinar the screen is all you see. You dictate the pace. The voice is yours and only yours. Okay, apart from the moderator.

I took a normal PowerPoint presentation as the software for my webinar. Thank goodness I had a practice mock webinar rehearsal the week before broadcast. I fluffed my lines, dried up, panicked, un-panicked, lost the plot and felt so small I could squeeze through a crack in the floorboards. When my blood pressure finally fell to normal levels this is what I learned:

1. Use an opening chart to tell people what you're going to talk about.
2. Clearly define the ground you want to cover, outline the structure and content so your audience knows what to expect – and of course, prepare and know the content well.
3. Use visual charts – pictures or images, as many as necessary as every picture tells a story.
4. Keep text slides to a minimum.
5. Don't overcomplicate chart text – short and sweet – plain language – avoid jargon and acronyms.
6. Insert 'link' slides between topics to allow listeners to adjust to the next up-and-coming subject.

7. The link slides give you as presenter time to take a sip of water – otherwise, after 15 minutes or so you'll literally 'dry-up'.
8. Slow down when talking – don't rush, even though the adrenalin may be pumping. Generally make the participants feel you're talking 'to' them not 'at' them.
9. Use of the pause is also important to let people assimilate the information or refocus before you tell them something new or important.
10. Keep the whole webinar as short and tight as possible – think of yourself as the person listening and judge how long it would take for your attention to wane.
11. Use visualisation software to convert data into graphically interesting images. This makes presenting figures easier on the eyes and on the brain.
12. Introduce subject polls to stimulate audience interaction and give yourself a few welcome seconds to draw breath.
13. Prepare a couple of questions the moderator can ask you to get the Q&A section started.

On the day, it went better than I'd hoped. Mistakes were made – but aren't they always? In webinars definitely 'less is more'. The less to worry about, the better the delivery. One thing, if you're reading from a script it will be noticed. Practise, practise, rehearse, rehearse, then let the actual event take care of itself. These are the extra things I learned:

1. Vocal Warm-up

The important connection with the previous chapters was that I did not warm up properly. I needed to concentrate on relaxing my mind and body and warming up my voice. My presentation was to last for about 45 minutes. These were not 45 minutes during which I was interacting with people but 45 minutes of non-stop talking. It placed a considerable strain on my voice. I had to break away in mid-sentence to take a drink of water and allow my vocal chords to recover for a second. I knew I had about 23 people signed up to the webinar and I was creating a dead space of silence and keeping them waiting. Luckily I managed to say that I would be taking a quick drink and asked them to examine the slide I'd left in place.

2. Human Contact

I was given a great introduction by the moderator. This did include a personal photo so the audience would know what I looked like. The feedback in my case was via the moderator who hosted the Q&A session. So I answered the question, talking into the microphone without hearing any response from a person. That takes a little getting used to. It is best to regularly check to see if everyone understands what you are saying.

3. Invest in a Microphone Headset

Using a headset unit of earphones and voice microphone is really worth the investment. An open mic standing on your desk not only picks up ambient sound like doors banging or people talking in the background but it lacks definition if you are moving around in your seat or if you head is bobbing to and fro as you speak into it. Also, if you are using your mouse with one hand to change slides your vocal direction will change too. If you can, use a remote to click the charts to make a smoother transition between slides.

4. Keep the Slides Engaging

Try to be as creative as you can with the slides you use. The screen and what's on it will draw the total focus of your audience. If you've got charts to present, construct the information brick by brick so each piece of information overlays and explains the points you're trying to make. Use pictures as visual hooks with a spoken narrative complementing the message contained in the image.

5. Clock Watch

Keep an eye on the time. When you rehearse, time the different sections and factor-in Q&A time during the delivery and at the end of the webinar.

6. Voice Watch

Use all you've learnt about pitching and placing your voice to make sure your presentation is not one monotonous drone. Mix up the delivery with pauses between spoken sections. Make your voice in its tone and inflections something that is easy on the ear. You can take a breath between the narrative sweeps and use silence to emphasise a point.

7. Two-way Traffic

As you move from point to point, encourage involvement and interaction by asking rhetorical questions, in the absence of having a one-to-one conversation, like:

"I bet you've experienced that before in your business", "Don't tell me you're already doing that", "If you've got any queries or want to explore something that's of particular interest to your organisation, I'd be happy to help after the webinar".

8. Close Out

Leave time at the end to deliver a prepared closing statement. This may be by way of a summary, a recap of key points, but try to leave them with some key learning outcomes to close down the webinar. The end is often the beginning of a new business relationship, or this may be the presentation that gets you noticed and further enhances your career prospects. Make sure you leave your contact details.

9. Photo Focus

Have a photo of a person about a foot away from you so you can focus on them while you talk – this helps to direct your voice in a consistent direction and stops you drifting off vocally.

10. Webcam Secret Reveals

If you're using Skype or video-call webinars, the webcam may reveal more than you intended! Take these points into consideration:

- It's important to consider where you are situated in a room or office and to consider your lighting. Don't sit with your back to a window or you will be a silhouette.
- Check that your jacket or something similar isn't hanging on the back of the door you just shut to make the room quiet and give you some privacy.
- Another thing that I have seen is a speaker who had lots of bags hanging on the back of a door off-camera that banged every time someone came into the room.

Oh, and make sure the camera is positioned so the audience isn't looking up your nose…

2. Online Video Presentation

Video already is, and will become *even more*, central to business communications in the coming years. The development of 4G phone technology has produced high-definition video for everyday use. Video is increasingly being embedded in electronic CVs and resumes or as stand-alone mini-films to promote a person or product. That's on top of the variety of applications that have become second nature to us via You Tube or video sharing sites like Vimeo. Websites are questioned if they do not use video to capture attention and relate core messages quickly and professionally. With video prominence growing daily, developing your skills in using the medium to promote your business or to present video yourself is the subject of this section.

There is a bewildering amount of statistical evidence quoted online supporting the power of video. As soon as they've been posted they are out of date. To the marketer it is the principles that are important – figures will alter overnight but these essential points will stand the test of time:

- The brain processes pictures and images 60,000 times faster than written text
- Research has shown that people will spend twice as long on a webpage if it carries video
- 80% of internet users watch video online – and this is bound to grow
- Videos are shared easily and quickly across a wide range of media at no extra cost. The power and flexibility of video makes it a fundamental element in business communications.

However…

'Everyone can do it.' But not everybody can do it well. Here's Peter Cooke of Dudleigh Films to take you through the process of preparing for and executing a professional video performance.

Peter Cooke of Dudleigh Films

You've heard the phrase 'One picture is worth a thousand words'. Statisticians tell us that one minute of video is worth 1.8 million words or 1,800 pictures, if you apply this to the ancient Chinese saying. Whatever way you look at it, that's a lot of images, images you can use to broadcast yourself or your company.

For video to make a real impact it needs to be short, engaging and informative. Once attention is captured, the call to action must seal the conversation. The maximum length of a video should be 90 seconds. Up to 60 seconds, if punchy and captivating, is good. The first 10 seconds are vital.

This does not mean you have to bedazzle viewers with stunning effects or have a sound track that leaps from the speakers like audio dynamite. The quality and relevance of your message to your target audience must be your starting point. Video production, like all presentations is a process you're already familiar with.

1. Define your business or personal objectives. A video can take the form of a simple piece to camera or a video that demonstrates a process or shows the advantages of your product or service.
2. Think of your viewers – use the 'What's in it for me' principle. What benefit will your video be to them. Look at the project through their eyes.
3. Decide whether you are going solo and making the video yourself or involving people who can mentor you through the production and performance, editing and formatting for video sharing.
4. Prepare a shooting script and storyboard if required – planning is central to a successful outcome.
5. Think about including filmed testimonials from your client customers. There is nothing more convincing than satisfied customers sharing their positive experience.
6. Create a project path with a timing plan and budget allowance. If going solo this may mean sourcing an HD camera, lapel microphone, lights and tripod or flexible attachment like a 'Gorilla' pod.

7. High-quality HD video can now be shot with most smartphones, but it is advisable to use an inexpensive lapel microphone to improve the audio quality. Brackets are available to mount your phone onto a tripod. Always use the phone in 'landscape' as opposed to 'portrait'. Do not film with a bright or distracting background to your subject. Ensure that the subject is well lit.

8. Music can greatly enhance the impact of your message and the viewing experience. Make sure you source royalty-free music. There are a number of sites providing excellent music including premiumbeat.com and musicbakery.com.

Tips on Video Performance

Like most things, the more you practise, the better you'll get. It will probably take time for you to feel comfortable in front of the camera. You will become familiar with the way you look and sound on-screen. Make time to practise by looking into and talking to your webcam and take note of the way you start to relax and 'get over yourself'. If you feel uptight this will come across. If you practise by using camera (as opposed to a webcam), look directly into the LENS of the camera – not in the direction of the whole camera but into the circular lens itself as if you're speaking to someone inside the camera. When you begin to record:

- Relax, smile, put on a 'welcoming' face. Pretend you're talking to a friend or someone you know
- Wear appropriate clothing
- Bring your personality into the shoot. Be natural as suits the occasion. Change expressions and change the tone and volume of your voice to mix up the delivery
- Slow down your delivery – speak at a rate that allows you to concentrate on diction and clarity of voice.

Writing a Shooting Script

Let's assume a shooting script for a 60-second video. This will call for a *maximum* of 120 words. Unlike the elevator pitches where you talk non-stop, in video you will have to factor in pauses for:

- Using light and shade in your vocal delivery when speaking
- Adding images or data as part of the presentation
- Adding music sound-bed.

When writing your script, use simple language and practise any names, phrases or business terms that could tongue-tie you. I advise my clients to imagine that they are delivering a presentation to a group of friends and then record the audio. This recording can then be transcribed and tweaked to provide your final script. When delivered to camera it will sound like the 'real' you. Read your script out loud, edit it and rehearse it until it flows smoothly. A teleprompter can greatly improve the delivery of a piece to camera. Low-cost teleprompters are available for use with iPads and smartphones, although they do require a little practice to start with.

10

HOW TO HANDLE MEDIA INTERVIEWS

Media interviews are a two-way street. You'll have information or breaking news to impart; the media want a story. If you consider this to be a form of negotiation where both parties have their own agendas then you'll enter the exchange with eyes wide open and brain fully engaged. The benefits in terms of both personal and corporate public relations can be substantial, especially if you become known as one of the go-to people for expert advice. Gaining the status of a go-to person means you have built a relationship and gained the trust of the media. You are trusted to impart correct and accurate information. Also, the expectation is that you will provide personal comment that would be of interest to their media audience.

The repercussions of bad press due to poor performance are legendary. This is why it is vital to prepare, practise and perform professionally.

Steve Hyland and Linda Bazant, Managing Directors of Business Connections Live and Retail Therapy Television

Steve and Linda have created a state-of-the art programme production and media training facility for business. A major part of their work is to coach people who have little or no experience with the media to prepare them for the challenge. This involves training to use equipment confidently for radio and television as well as advice on how to prepare yourself and anticipate media questions.

If you appreciate the needs of the media and the pressures they may be under to deliver a story to their editors you can equip yourself better for the expected and unexpected.

Preparation and Anticipation

Even though the form of media interviews may be different the essentials remain constant. The more you think 'ahead of time' the more prepared you'll be, particularly if you anticipate 'left-field' questions; these are *surprise* topical questions or ones on the margin of your expertise in which a reporter asks your opinion. Check the media for breaking stories and check on company policy before you say something you'll regret.

Interviews may result from a reporter wanting more information after receiving a PR release. Reporters may be from a specialist business magazine, local or national media, radio, television or digital platforms. Each part of the media will have a different approach and perhaps a different agenda. The first contact is often a phone call, with the intention of conducting the interview over the phone or to arrange a person-to-person meeting or agree a radio or TV studio date. If a reporter suggests a telephone interview, don't begin if you have not prepared properly. Buy time and arrange a future date.

A reporter may want to develop their own interesting angle to the story. In a business scenario it is wise to prepare for questions related to:

- Your particular field of expertise – that will probably be the reason you have been contacted in the first place. For example, a PR release.
- Your company and its operations – especially if your market segment is in the news for any reason
- Wider business related issues
- Your reaction to any breaking news in politics or wider issues that could be newsworthy.

Back-up Sources

Expect reporters to frame questions stemming from the basic formula: *Who, What, When, Where, Why and How?* That's why you'll need to gather 'evidence' to verify your answers. Become knowledgeable about supporting facts so you can provide back-up to statements or opinions and quote your sources if necessary.

General Preparation Check List

About You
- Decide your message priorities – where you can make positive points
- What do you want to achieve as a result of the interview?
- Prioritise your key messages – write them down in order
- Develop short phrases and keywords – sound-bite sentences
- Anticipate questions – easy-hard-really difficult ones
- Practise responses to areas that are off-limits – say if information is private
- Gather your supporting evidence and be fluent in facts and figures
- Remove jargon – keep your answers simple and easy to explain – avoid ambiguity
- Prepare visuals and documents for the use of the media
- Prepare anecdotes – business stories to bring your responses alive
- Rehearse and keep calm – grasp the opportunity for great results
- Summary statement – prepare key ideas and phrases to end your interview
- Check on venue, arrival time and travel time – allowing a margin for delays

Remember the 'Rather Rule' attributed to the veteran CBS News Anchor Dan Rather:

"There are only three legitimate answers to a reporter's question:

1. Yes, I know the answer and here it is.
2. No, I don't know the answer but I'll try to find out.
3. Yes, I do know the answer, but I can't tell you."

About Them

- Get name and contact details of the media outlet
- Assess their editorial aims and objectives
- Try to find out in advance what the interviewer is interested in – see if you can research any other pieces they've written to determine their stance
- Who is their target audience?
- When do they expect the piece to be published – when will the story run?
- What is the interview length going to be and what form will it take?
- Is the interview to be held in your offices or another venue or studio?
- Consider whether you can build a future relationship
- Don't ask to pre-approve the article
- However, you could contact your interviewer after the interview by phone or email to recap on your key points and invite them to contact you if they need any clarification

During the Interview

The more involved and positive you are, the more likely the interview is to produce opportunities to put your points across in a way that favours your position. Here are some pointers and techniques to help the experience be a productive one.

On Duty – Off the Record

In Rugby Union there's a phrase: 'body in the oven – brain in the fridge'. No matter how excited you are your brain has to be ice-cold, precise and alert. You're on duty. Do not misjudge the moment and say things 'off the record' as nothing is off the record in an interview situation.

Be pleasant, be friendly, be charming but don't let your guard down.

Flag-Up Key Points

Flagging or headlining key points in advance makes the interviewer aware you are about to share something important. You may use phrases like these as flags:

"But the important thing to note is…"
"The key point is that…"
"The one essential point I would like to make clear is…"

Bridge Gaps

Bridging is a technique to manoeuvre the conversation away from something you don't want to speak about to something you do. The bridging statement takes you over to firmer ground, such as:

"That's interesting, but have you thought about…"
"Yes, but have you considered this…"
"I think what you really want to know about is…"
"The really key thing here is…"

'No Comment'; Don't Say This, Block the Question Instead

This is not a police interview. If you say those two words you will kill the conversation stone dead. The more acceptable way is to indicate why you cannot answer the question, for example:

> *"I'm sorry, I am not able to answer your question here and now but I will try to get back to you…"*
> *"I should explain that this relates to company policy and I am not in a position to speak on this matter…"*
> *"I believe a statement on this matter will be released officially shortly…"*

Counter-Strike Answers

A way to reinforce your position is to tag your answer with a link to one of your key points. For example:

> *"(short answer) this links directly to our objective of…"*
> *"(short answer) this reinforces our view that…"*
> *"(short answer) this supports our position of…"*

Tell Stories

Use metaphors, anecdotes and business stories to liven-up your contribution and add emphasis to the points you wish to make. This could include business case studies presented as engaging stories. It is particularly important with radio to paint a picture with words for the listening audience. There's a phrase, 'see it on the radio', and your role is to bring your descriptions to life for the listener.

Hot Spots – Under Pressure

There may be times when an interviewer deliberately heats up the interchange to pressure you into making mistakes or revealing too much or just to rattle your cage. Keep calm and recognise what's happening when:

a) **Rapid fire questions** are shot at you in a single assault. Stay still and wait until the barrage is over. Then say something along the lines of:
"(say name of interviewer) There were a number of different questions just then. Which one would you like to me to answer first?"
or
"So many questions; I'll try to answer them all for you but how long have we got, and where would you like me to start?"

b) **The interviewer makes summarising mistakes.** If an interviewer attempts to sum-up or paraphrase what you've said but gets it wrong – intentionally or not – then try:
"I'm sorry, I think you must have misheard me. What I actually said was…"
and correct the mistake. You can interrupt to stop the mistake being accepted as right.

c) **You're interrupted.** You can continue to speak if you can put your point across or politely ask to be allowed to finish what you were saying. Interviewers use interruptions to steer the conversation back to their agenda or to catch you off guard with a contentious question. In this situation play for time so you can devise a response, for example:
"If you'd let me finish my point first I will attempt to answer your new question."

Personal Profiles

Prepare a short descriptive piece on you as a person. This will include your business role but also introduce you as a human being with interests and achievements. This could include 'something that people don't know about me, to put a little flesh on your business bones.

Here are the preparation sheets we produce at Business Connections Live for Radio and TV interviews.

General Interview Summary Checklist and Preparation

Interview Details	• Date and Time of Interview • Reporter • Contact Information • Media Outlet/Publication
Story Statement	• Have a general introduction to your perspective of the topic at hand. • Use plain language. • Keep it short.
Topic	• For each topic to be covered, have supporting evidence and incorporate key messages.
Wrap Statement	• Generally sum up your main points and your perspective. • Make it a strong statement and include a 'quotable quote'.
Consider the Medium	• Support your story. TV is pictures, so consider visuals that enhance your story. • Wear appropriate clothes (e.g. don't wear white, green or complicated patterns). • For radio, think about appropriate use of tone of voice/emotion/silence that will enhance your presentation delivery.

Giving a Radio Interview – Summary Checklist and Preparation

Preparation	• Find out as much as you can about the programme on which you are being asked to appear. Is it live or taped? • What angle are they taking? What are they expecting from you? What questions do you think they might ask? • Is the audience completely general or specialised? • What are your key messages? Think about the points you could make which are most interesting, useful and relevant to the appropriate audience. Think of a quote you could deliver. • Fill out an Interview Prep Form. • Role-play in advance.
Key Message/s	• When preparing for the interview, think about your key messages. • During the interview, use every opportunity to re-state these messages.
Speak Normally	• Think about the way you talk in your work life. Do you normally use a lot of technical terms and other jargon? • A general audience won't understand you and, probably, neither will the interviewer. • Avoid too many facts and figures as your audience will never remember them and will most likely tune out. • Find creative ways of explaining something. Imagine that you are chatting with someone who is perfectly intelligent but who simply doesn't know anything at all about your subject. How would you explain it to them without being patronising? • Do not write down answers ahead of time. However, you might want to use 'prompt' words, printed in an easy-to-read font.

'Work' the Medium	When you are preparing for a radio interview, think of ways to enhance and work with the special qualities of radio, e.g. paint verbal pictures, tell short anecdotes that illustrate a point, use appropriate emotion. Think of the 'story' you want to tell.
Prepare Sound Bites	Few radio 'sound bites' are more than 20 seconds long. Develop and rehearse some key quotes in advance that will fit this format. Consider mentioning your company's name or your department in the sound bite to ensure that your affiliation with your company is not edited out of the story. The inclusion of a website can be very powerful (without the www).
Sit Comfortably	Avoid tight-fitting clothes. Keep your feet flat on the floor and sit in a comfortable chair. Avoid chairs with wheels or chairs that rock.
Avoid Nervous Habits	Avoid habits such as 'ums' and 'ahs' or clearing your throat. Avoid paper shuffling. Keep a glass of water on hand.
No Comment	If you use this phrase, the viewer or listener is likely to jump to the conclusion that you are evasive or untrustworthy. Find a way to answer the question using positive messages. Tell the truth. If you don't know the answer, say so – never guess at an answer.
No Confrontation	Be honest and friendly. Even if it feels as if you are under attack, don't lose your temper and don't sound defensive. Stick to positive statements and never resort to negative statements or critical attacks. Don't be afraid to admit mistakes. Remind yourself that reporters are often looking for the sexy, juicy angle. The story you want to tell may not be the story they want to tell.
Evaluate Yourself	No interview is ever perfect. It's good to evaluate your performance so that you continue to improve. Ask your friends and colleagues for feedback – ask them what they thought your main point was and compare that to the key message(s) you intended to project. Did you sound conversational?

TV Interview Techniques – Summary Checklist and Preparation

Confirm Details	Find out as much as you can about the appearance ahead of time: • Confirm whether the programme is live or taped and if it will or will not be edited • Consider the programme format (talk show, news, variety, panel, call-in). If a panel, find out who the other panellists are and points they will be making • Ask if there is a studio audience and audience make-up (specialised, general) • Find out the interview length. The shorter the interview, the more critical it is that you condense your main messages into sound bites of 10 to 20 seconds • Ask the pre-interviewer what their expectations of you are; what type of angles on the topic at hand are they looking for? Make sure the opinion you have to offer is one in which they are interested.
Key Message(s)	Think about what you want to communicate to the audience ahead of time. Write down your key messages in advance. Draft concise, to-the-point statements, or 'sound bites' that highlight these points. • During the interview, take the opportunity to re-state these messages. • Think about the one quote or message you want the audience to remember. • Use analogies, related stories and personal experiences to help everyone understand your point of view. • If the interviewer or reporter is coming to your location, create a visually enhancing environment to help emphasize your message. Use props or stage a working environment.

Prepare	Prepare, prepare, prepare! Even a bit of preparation will go a long way towards achieving an effective and compelling interview.
	<ul><li>Fill out an Interview Prep Form.</li><li>Role-play in advance.</li><li>Practise delivering your sound bites and examples in a mock interview with a colleague or friend – or even in front of a mirror.</li><li>Practise delivering each of your answers in less than 20 seconds.</li><li>Prepare for worst-case questions.</li><li>Keep an eye on current events related to your topic, especially if the story is breaking news.</li></ul>
Be Comfortable	If you are comfortable during the interview, you and your messages will come across much more effectively. Try some of the following to help put you at ease before and during the interview.
	<ul><li>Arrive at least 30 minutes early for interviews held at a studio.</li><li>Arrange to meet the interviewer or reporter before the programme whenever possible and ask how you will address each other during the programme (i.e. first name basis?).</li><li>Adjust and test any equipment before the programme begins. If you are speaking into a microphone, maintain a distance of at least six inches.</li><li>If it is a long interview, ask for a glass of water on the set. Avoid cola, chocolate, and dairy products.</li><li>Choose a comfortable chair that doesn't swivel.</li></ul>

Follow Best Practices	A few essentials for giving a great interview: • Be yourself. Be natural. • Speak in lay terms. Don't use any technical language or industry jargon. • Assume that you will be on the air for every second of the programme. Don't make a gesture or say something you don't want broadcast. • Assume that anything you say to the reporter could be brought into the interview, even if it's a casual remark made during a pre-taping chat. • Keep the audience profile in mind. • Direct your remarks to the audience. • Look at the reporter, not the camera. • Limit your answers to about three sentences..
Avoid Bad Practices	Try to avoid the following: • Don't look at the monitor during the interview. • Don't speak for someone who isn't present. • Don't let any misleading statements trap you. • Avoid nervous habits. • Never fill in 'dead' time – that's the interviewer's job.
TV is Pictures	Unlike radio, TV is a medium of images. Your visual appearance can help with the success of the interview; a few simple things can make a big difference: • Wear comfortable clothing. Bright/pastel solid colours look best on camera. Avoid small, busy patterns or shiny fabrics. Don't wear overpowering scarves or ties. • Avoid wearing large, dangling, shiny jewellery. • Makeup, powder and lipstick will help you avoid looking 'washed out' by the bright lights. • Comb your hair. • Check your appearance on the TV monitor beforehand, if possible.

Avoid Confrontation	A negative, nasty tone can kill an interview. Try to remember the following and you will be able to handle any negative situation that can arise during an on-air discussion: • Don't get into an argument. • If the reporter's tone turns nasty, don't match it. Stick to positive statements and messages. • Never become defensive or angry. Maintain your composure at all times. • Keep to your own agenda by answering each question with a direct, factual statement followed by a relevant key message. • Don't be afraid to admit mistakes. A useful phrase is: "What I can tell you is… "
Never say Never	• Never say, "No comment." • Never offer any information 'off the record' or 'just between you and me'.
Evaluate Yourself	No interview is ever perfect. It's good to evaluate your performance so you continue to improve. Ask your friends and colleagues for feedback. Ask them what they thought your main point was and compare that to the key message(s) you intended to project. Did you sound conversational?

SPEECH!
GIVING A SPEECH FOR BUSINESS OR AT A PERSONAL EVENT LIKE A WEDDING

Keep Panic – Don't Calm!

Panicking is a natural first reaction. Don't worry, your brain will sort you out. All you need to do is keep calm and don't panic.

As with all the advice in the first chapters, the key is to prepare for the challenge, whether you have to deliver a speech in a business environment or your best mate has asked you to be his best man – turn this sentence around if your best friend has asked you to be her best woman. The situations may be different but the initial thought processes are the same. What do I say and how do I say it?

In both scenarios, be yourself. Nobody expects you to suddenly perform like a Hollywood film star or a seasoned television presenter. Be true to yourself and remain grounded. Your audience of work colleagues or guests at a wedding breakfast want to hear what you have to say, want to learn something or be entertained. They will be supportive. Don't doubt yourself.

Reasons to Believe

It is not only a question of what you say but how much you mean it. It will be clear to everyone that you've worked hard to produce a speech especially for them to instruct, to change perceptions, to inspire or raise their spirits, make them laugh and fill their hearts with joy. They will thank you for the gift of learning or love you've given them. Where do we start?

Step by Step for a Business Speech

In business a 3-stage speech structure is a solid base on which to start creating your speech.

1. An introduction – where you tell them what you are about to tell them
2. A middle section – where you cover the detail and supporting information
3. A final round-up – where you repeat the key points and make a summary and 'Call to Action' to get things done and leave the audience energised.

Starting a speech is the scariest part. You have to connect with the audience. To do this you have to have to answer the audience's question: 'What's in it for me – why should I pay attention – why should I listen to this speech?'

Answering this question is a starting point for your research and preparation. It will help you create a great start to your speech; in short, start by explaining the **end** benefit of their involvement.

These examples are purely to give you an idea of the kind of approach.

Start with the end benefit:
"Today, I'm going to explain how your lives are going to change for the better."
Then follow with a rhetorical question:
"How does that sound? Interested? Knowing that in an hour's time, when you walk out of this room, you will be different people?"

Or start with a question:
"Hands up, how many of you want to spend more time relaxing than working?"
Then explain a new way of working that reduces boring, time-consuming tasks.

Or start with a story:
"Are you all settled? Then I'm going to tell you a story."

Tell them a real-life story that may or may not be a business story but has a link to your speech content. Concentrate on stories about people – people who may be like those in your audience.

Or start with a startling fact:
"Vending machines kill four times as many people as sharks do per year" or *"The average four year-old child asks over 400 questions a day"* or *"Humans shed 40 pounds of skin in their lifetime, completely replacing their outer skin every month"* or *"More than 2,500 left-handed people are killed every year using equipment meant for right-handed people."* (Note: The author is left-handed!)

Big Finish

There are as many ways to wrap up and close your speech. Here are a few of them.

1. Closing the Circle: This is where you end the theme of the speech in the same way you started. It could be by using the title to say something like:
   "We've now arrived at the same place we began. The journeys we've taken together have moved us on – so where do we go from here?"

2. The Challenge: If the speech is linked to people working together to take action on a project or to achieve an ongoing target the end piece could be a direct call to action:
   "We now know what has to be done. We know the importance of achieving the objective for us all, for the business and our families. Let's work together and smash it out of the park."

3. The Killer Quotation: Choose something that resonates with the audience. This does not have to be from someone from history. It could be taken from a song, a film screenplay or a sporting hero. For example:

"As Muhammad Ali the Greatest said, 'Don't count the days – make the days count'".

Or choose one that is brilliant. This is from Oscar Wilde: *"Be yourself – everyone else is taken."*

4. The Question Left Hanging: Asking a question and leaving it hanging for the audience to answer, either in their minds or by showing support and speaking out, can work really well, especially if the question links with a previous call to action.

    "The question as you leave here today is: are we going to rise to the challenge?"

Business Speech Tips

- Appear confident – even if you're not. Appearances and reality can be different things.
- Stand still at the front centre. Don't move. By being calm and in position you project authority.
- Warm up your voice beforehand.
- Get attention – sometimes standing and saying nothing and looking out to back, sides and front of the audience is enough to bring people to order.
- Practise using a microphone so you don't have it too close to your mouth.
- Use one of the starter techniques to surprise and capture attention – *"Did you know that more people in the world today suffer from obesity than hunger."*
- AFTER you've got their attention, introduce yourself and link what you used as your amazing opening statement. You could do it the conventional way by introducing yourself first. This is your call depending on your audience and how really confident you feel.
- Speak slower than your normal pace to allow the audience's ears to tune into your voice.
- Raise and lower your voice. Increase or reduce the volume to emphasise a point.
- Use silence as punctuation. Pauses create breathing spaces to allow people to absorb what has been said.
- Use interesting props to surprise, entertain and stimulate thinking. Be creative.
- If you're using presentation software, use images to tell a story. The brain

processes pictures much faster than it processes text on a screen. Using pictures as a hook allows you as presenter to have the ace up your sleeve as you are the only one who knows what the point is you're going to make.

- If you have text on a chart keep it short and simple – add another chart rather than cram in too many words.
- Smile and change your facial expressions. Open your arms. Show the palms of your hands. Reach out.
- Ask people in the audience to contribute, ask questions, ask for their opinions, ask them whether they understood what you've just said. Use feedback as links bridging to your next point or subject.
- When writing a speech, say the words out loud. Often words on a page don't sound right as they come out of your mouth. Use simple words, short sentences and short bursts of information before pausing to make sure your audience has kept up with you.
- Repeat yourself. Repetition reinforces learning. Say the same thing again immediately or at other points in the presentation – use the repeated line or lines as glue to stick the learning together. Repetition forces a message home.
- Show them you care. Use language that is emotive. Project feeling to your audience. Let them know this is not just another talk – you're there to make a difference.

A Speech to Family and Friends

The Wedding Speech

This is the speech that could make you run for cover; the best man's or best woman's speech. Either colour drains from your face at the thought of it or you smile and say, "Bring it on!" There are general tips in this piece that will help you prepare for other private occasions too. These notes are written for wedding or civil partnerships; please make adjustments to suit those involved, whatever gender.

Traditionally, the accepted order of speeches at the end of the wedding breakfast/meal (in some countries the wedding meal is called the wedding breakfast) is:

1. The Bride's Father – to include a toast to the bride and groom
2. The Bridegroom – primarily to thank all those who helped to make the day a success, especially a thank you to the bridesmaids. A second toast to the bridesmaids. The groom's speech could be longer if desired
3. The Best Man's or Woman's Speech – responds on behalf of the bridesmaids. I mention a Best Woman's speech as it is not unheard of for a woman to deliver the speech if the Best Man is quaking in his boots and is incapable of standing up and delivering a speech. It goes without saying that the speech givers will reflect the nature of the wedding or civil partnership. The speech tips are relevant to all speakers. This speech is the centrepiece of speeches. A further toast to the happy couple completes the speeches unless…
4. Bride's Speech – many brides choose to make their own special contribution. It is the bride's prerogative to cover any aspect of the speeches or event she wishes. A further toast is definitely likely!

Key Duties of the Best Man/Best Woman

- Organise the Stag/Hen Night
- Go to the rehearsal
- Look after the groom/bride before the ceremony
- Drive him/her to the wedding – arrive early
- Take responsibility for the rings. Put them somewhere safe and easy-to-access on your person
- Escort the groom/bride to the ceremony

- Sign the register
- Deliver the key speech
- Flirt with the bridesmaids
- Dance 'til dawn

Creating your Speech

The keynote speech must include the groom and the bride. It is to be a celebration of their union. Naturally it is essential to poke fun at the groom and recall humorous stories from the past; stories that are entertaining and full of incident but NOT raunchy or in bad taste or that will embarrass everyone and reflect badly on you. No mention of past relationships. No bad language. Keep the speech as long as you can easily handle. You could consider this structure. Our players are Brian – best man, John – the dashing groom and Karen, his gorgeous bride.

1. Introduce yourself to the wedding party. *"I'm Brian; I've known John since we were learning to walk. My first duty is to say a big thanks to the beautiful bridesmaids. Can we raise our glasses to* (name the bridesmaids)."
2. After the bridesmaids toast, read out messages of congratulations from cards, emails or texts. You could include a couple that you've made up as joke messages from John's sporting heroes.
3. Switch attention to the groom: *"What can I say about John"*
4. Tell a couple of stories about the groom – be careful of telling jokes unless you're an expert. A possible linking line is: *"Not many of you know this but…"*
5. Introduce the point when John met Karen and how you noticed a change come over him and how his attention switched from his favourite sport or hobby, for example, if he is a keen angler: *"Before he met Karen, John's idea of love was looking deep into the eyes of a 17-pound Carp"* or *"John's idea of romance was not candlelight and soft music but watching* (sports team name goes here) *under floodlights and hearing the ref's whistle blow."* See if you can find some hilarious props to support this section of the speech. If you feel confident enough you can project images on a screen or use music clips to tie in the point you're making.

6. After this, link to the bride.
7. Compliment the bride and say how stunning she looks.
8. Ask for everyone to charge their glasses and stand to wish John and Karen a life full of laughter, love and misbehaviour.

Song lyrics or lines from favourite movies, or quotes from celebrities, are all sources of material to add to your speech.

> "Basically my wife was immature. I'd be at home in the bath and she'd come in and sink my boats." – Woody Allen
> "I don't think my wife likes me very much; when I had a heart attack she wrote for an ambulance." – Frank Carson

Delivering the Speech
- Stay sober.
- Use notes if you want to – don't try to do it all without referring to notes.
- Warm up your voice – keep a glass of water handy.
- Allow time for the audience to enjoy the jokes.
- Speak loud enough to be heard by everyone – don't shout down the microphone.
- Rehearse and time yourself – in front of a mirror if that works for you.
- The event may be videoed so be aware of the camera.
- Be true to yourself.
- Remember your speech will live in the memory of the bride and groom.

Other Occasions
Speeches on retirement and at leaving dos, acceptance speeches and eulogies are all part of the cycle of speeches. Giving thanks is probably the one element that ties them together. Thanks to the people you work with, to those who've helped you achieve a goal, or thanks to family and friends. In each of these scenarios, concentrate on people and personal stories to connect with your listeners.

CHAPTER 12

SOCIAL MEDIA
THE CONVERSATION CONTINUES

No book on communication skills would be complete without mentioning the power and influence of social media. Not so long ago, social media was a distant relation to business and conventional communication media. Now it is at its heart. This contribution by Mark Hughes explains the growing influence of social media for business and also as a necessary skill for the fully rounded communicator. Using social media polishes your communication skills, making you more capable and more confident.

Mark Hughes – Social Media Specialist

Social Media as a Communication Engine

When it comes to collaboration and information distribution, social media is a great way to involve employees and brand ambassadors from all positions and levels within your organisation with the purpose of sharing news, information and resources. Tools such as Twitter, Facebook and LinkedIn allow organisations to speak directly to and solicit responses from the public marketplace, as well as from their employees, quickly and affordably.

Social media is one of the best opportunities for effective communication in the digital world and is often regarded as the best way to build or grow relationships on the internet. The most effective social media platforms for professional communication are Facebook, Twitter and LinkedIn. Facebook is the most complete social experience and incorporates photos, videos, messaging and virtual groups.

Twitter is perfect for brief conversations and reaching out to people you may or may not know. LinkedIn is essentially the business version of Facebook and is a great way to network within your industry or career field.

10 Ways to Benefit from Social Media

1. **Unlock Institutional Knowledge and Expertise**
   Internal blogs, forums and social networks allow organisations to unlock institutional knowledge by allowing employees to share questions, answers and valuable information in open forums rather than the confines of email, where only a few people benefit from shared information. Employees can stay abreast of the most up-to-date information and employers can identify staff needs.

2. **Unleash Creativity, Diverse Thinking and Innovation**
   Constant idea-sharing in a cutting-edge environment creates a culture of innovation and collaboration. Social media allows organisations to easily conduct virtual brainstorms and focus groups by tapping into a broad base of diverse thinking and creativity.

3. **Generate Leads and Revenue**
   Sharing marketing messages and offers with employees in easy-to-pass-along formats can help employees accurately advocate for your products and services, generate leads and boost the bottom line.

4. **Improve Speed, Agility and Efficiency**
   The ability to communicate with employees in real time can help organisations educate employees, distribute facts, quash misinformation

and respond to urgent employee needs. This speed is especially critical for crisis communications – both inside and outside your organisation.

5. **Strengthen Culture and Employee Camaraderie**
   Frequent and timely communication helps employees stay plugged in to what's going on in the organisation. The ability to connect employees with similar talents and interests can also build stronger working relationships.

6. **Reduce Costs and Increase Productivity**
   Effective use of social media has a green benefit and can eliminate unnecessary paper printing and help employees interact more efficiently.

7. **Eliminate Regional and Global Communication Barriers**
   Social media helps employees communicate beyond borders and time zones, crossing continents for 24-hour communications between geographically dispersed teams.

8. **Make Information Mobile**
   Mobile-friendly communication allows organisations to communicate with employees anytime, anywhere, which can be particularly useful for a workforce that is frequently on the move or without computer access.

9. **Retain and Recruit Top Talent**
   Social media allows you to communicate more effectively with the next generation of employees, namely Millennials, for whom social media is standard practice.

10. **Lead with Clear Communication**
    All organisations must continually reinforce their missions, values and strategies to rally employees around a common cause. Social media provides endless opportunities to motivate employees in fresh and creative ways.

Social Media Impact

Multi-dimensional interactions have altered the basic rules of communication. Social media has drastically changed how we communicate. Not too long ago, we communicated through the mail, on a landline telephone and in person. Today, we send text messages; leave voice messages; use instant messenger; send emails; talk through headphones, mobile phones and online video phones and, of course, interact through the Internet, where a plethora of social media tools has redefined communication.

Such a redefinition has had an enormous effect. The entire paradigm of social media has altered the basic rules of communication, especially between businesses and their audiences. The one-way communication methods of the recent past, business-to-customer and business-to-business, have been replaced by a more robust multidimensional communication model. That model is collectively called social media (also referred to as Web 2.0).

What People Want

To communicate effectively in the social media world means understanding the new rules of the road. People want:
- To have a say
- To create a meaningful dialogue
- To be engaged and involved in the process
- To enjoy personal interactions with others
- To be listened to
- To help shape what they find useful
- To connect with others engaged in similar activities
- To talk plainly – for clear understanding
- For communication to be genuine and relevant
- To conduct business with ethical companies who work transparently
- To be in partnership.

Take Care

Take care if you're using social media while at work. Most companies have procedures in place as to what they allow or disallow staff in terms of how or even if they can use social media when in the workplace. Reputation management online is huge with larger corporations and one mistake or something said in jest but taken the wrong way could badly affect the business – and perhaps your job!

The 5 Cs – The Cornerstones of Social Media

Conversation

No longer is the communication one-way, broadcast or somehow sent to a passive audience. Social media is at least a two-way conversation and often a multidimensional conversation. Social media engages everyone involved.

Contribution

Social media encourages contributions and reactions from anyone who is interested. 'Encourage' is the key here; social media solicits an interaction, positive and negative, by making it easy to contribute.

Collaboration

Social media promotes an exchange of information between you and your audience, and among audience members, by inviting participation. Creating a quick and simple collaborative platform requires that information be organised and easily distributed.

Connection

Accessing information on the Internet only takes a click. Social media thrives on connections, within its own web vehicles and through links to other sites, resources, people and automatic feeds. People can even create their own personalised site of connections.

Community

The fundamental characteristic of social media is the creation of community: a fellowship and relationship with others who share common attitudes, interests and goals (such as friendship, professionalism, politics, and photography).

Communities form quickly and communicate effectively. Communities build goodwill from members to the hosting organisation and among members. While these communities are only virtual ones with members seldom meeting each other in person, they are no less robust than the physical communities in which we live, and in many ways they are more robust from the simple fact that barriers are removed.

SOCIAL MEDIA ETIQUETTE

Have you wondered exactly how to use LinkedIn for business? Here is advice on LinkedIn etiquette from the renowned Canadian social media expert Melonie Dodaro. Facebook, Twitter and other social media platforms have their own etiquette guide to online behaviour. If you show the same respect to others you won't go far wrong. Here's Melonie.

Melonie Dodaro
International #1 Bestselling Author of The LinkedIn Code, LinkedIn Expert,
Keynote Speaker, Social Selling Evangelist from Kelowna,
British Columbia, Canada

Has your fear of making mistakes prevented you from taking full advantage of all that the #1 business social network has to offer? This will help to demystify how to use LinkedIn for business by outlining some of the most tried and true methods that I've used to consistently generate more than 70% of my business on the network.

In this article you will discover the important dos and don'ts of LinkedIn etiquette and the mistakes you absolutely want to avoid making.

LinkedIn Etiquette: 10 Things You Must Do

1. Personalise Connection Requests

It's important to personalise all connection requests and avoid sending the default message like it's the black plague. There are many people on LinkedIn that don't appreciate random requests without a personal message. These are the example people who are likely to hit the 'Report Spam' or 'I Don't Know This Person' button. If that happens a few times, you'll be tossed into LinkedIn jail.

2. Have a Profile Picture

Don't start connecting with people until you have a professional photo of yourself. Your profile picture should be a nice, clean and professional headshot.

3. Keep it Personal

Sadly, there are many people who get in the habit of simply requesting a recommendation without adding a personal message. If you want to successfully receive recommendations from those who you know it's important to provide a personal note telling them that you are looking for one and always offer to reciprocate when appropriate.

4. Keep it Professional at All Times

Do not talk about anything that isn't relevant to business on LinkedIn – ever. LinkedIn is a business social network and people expect everything to be professional at all times.

5. Turn off Notifications when Updating Your Profile

Profile updates can get a bit annoying for your connections if you decide to make a lot of changes to your profile in one day. It's best to disable notifications when doing any profile updating for this reason.

6. Send a Welcome Message that Provides Value

One of the most critical steps in my LinkedIn marketing process is sending a welcome message to new connections to open up dialogue. Aim to provide them with some sort of value if you want to increase your odds of getting a response.

7. Regularly Nurture Relationships

Make an effort to reach out to your valued connections whenever it makes sense to nurture the relationship. It can be as easy as leaving a positive comment on their recent update, sending them useful content specific to their profession or even a simple congratulations for a promotion or a new product launch in their business. Success comes through selflessness. Trust me!

8. Make Your Contact List Open to Your Connections

It's important to open your contacts list up to your new connections; hiding them will have you seen as self-serving. When you connect with someone new you can see all of their contacts, what do you think they will feel about you if they see you have hidden your contacts?

9. Introduce Your Connections to Each Other

The best way to eventually gain referrals is by giving them to others. Be proactive with your business matchmaking and do the best you can to connect valuable connections with each other if you sense that there could be some synergy.

10. Respond Promptly to Messages

I like to treat LinkedIn etiquette similarly to email etiquette in this sense. One to two days for a response is perfectly acceptable but any longer is pushing the envelope.

LinkedIn Etiquette: 10 Things You Must NEVER Do

1. Don't Send Spammy Messages to Your Connections

The old saying *'Slow down the sale to speed it up'* fits well here and this means to not pitch by sending spammy, self-serving messages to your connections. Everything must always be positioned for their benefit, not yours.

2. Don't Over-Post

Avoid posting more than one status update per day on LinkedIn and definitely not more than two.

3. Don't Ask People You Don't Know for Recommendations

You should never ask for a recommendation (or give one) to someone that you can't personally vouch for. If someone with a poor reputation gives you a recommendation it will be put right on your profile, linking back to theirs. Yikes!

4. Don't Criticise or Comment Negatively in Groups

LinkedIn groups are a great place to make new connections but only if you don't turn them off with negativity. Don't be *that* guy (or girl)!

5. Do Not Post Self-Serving Content in Groups

LinkedIn groups are not for spamming your content. If you want to share your content then you need to craft it for the forum you want to post in and ensure that the goal of the content is to provide value *first*. Are you noticing a pattern yet?

6. Don't Send Messages to Multiple People without Unselecting this Option

If you are going to send a single message to reach multiple people you need to unselect the option that says 'Allow recipients to see each other's names and email addresses'. Nobody feels special getting a message that was carelessly sent to a bunch of other people.

7. Don't Ask People to Like Your Facebook Page

One of the biggest LinkedIn etiquette mistakes I see regularly is new, random connections begging for 'likes' on their Facebook page. It's really, *really* lame. It's totally different if, after building a relationship with someone, you also choose to connect with them personally on Facebook, but don't send a message saying, *"Please like my Facebook page."*

8. Don't Ask New Connections or People You Don't Know to Endorse You

Just because random people endorse you all the time doesn't make it okay to ask for endorsements if you don't know the person. I often get people that I don't know sending me messages saying, *"I just endorsed your skills can you endorse mine now?"* If they want to endorse you after they receive a notification that you endorsed them, they will; don't ask for it unless it's someone you know well.

9. Don't Send Messages with "I see you viewed my profile... "

In a word: creepy. If it's someone you want to connect with, go ahead and send a personalised connection request that does NOT include, "I see you viewed my profile."

10. Don't Treat LinkedIn Like Facebook or Twitter

LinkedIn etiquette is very different from Facebook and Twitter etiquette. It's important to know the appropriate etiquette for each network as they are often different – aka nobody wants to see what you ate for lunch on LinkedIn.

Last point: It's not about You, it's about Them

The biggest mistakes on social media come from the misconception that people care about what you have to say. That's simply not the case. They care about finding solutions to their problems, that's it.

The golden rule of LinkedIn etiquette and social media marketing in general is to always provide undeniable value that speaks to the exact type of person you are trying to connect with.

3 WRITING SKILLS

WRITING SKILLS INTRODUCTION

To make the most of improving your writing skills I've chosen to concentrate on those areas where the most value can be added. It stands to reason that the more practised you become, the more professional will be the result. All that you've learned in the previous sections will give you confidence to transform your communication performance, whether for business, career or personal use.

Let's begin by recapping on the essentials of communication in Section 1. These core elements remain constant for developing your writing skills, namely:

- Remember your central role as messenger is to make sure that there's no confusion but clear understanding of aims and objectives
- That each member of the business team is aware of the actions required of them individually
- Keep sentences and paragraphs short
- Use simple language, avoiding jargon and buzz words
- Be respectful and take nothing for granted, don't assume that every reader has a total understanding of the subject and acronyms
- Concentrate on the benefits you'll bring
- Do your research and speak from experience, refer to relevant evidence if needed
- Remember that your written word has to stand alone to be understood without you being there in person to explain any points
- Take time to think about the people who are likely to read your piece and make sure you've pitched the writing at the right seniority
- When writing for senior management – reports, requests, reviews – make sure you've satisfied the audience needs: the Visionaries, Dynamos and Questioners.

CHAPTER 13

MEMOS AND MINUTES

'Office memos are the product of a bygone age and a casualty of the digital age.'

True or false? It's false.

Memos are still a useful business tool even though they mostly arrive in an inbox rather than as a hard copy left in your in-tray. Memos help to organise and manage projects efficiently.

Well-written memos are a valuable method of:

- Communicating with a select team of people or a wider group within an organisation
- Reminding or alerting co-workers of a particular event or business development
- Helping to manage a project or projects with pertinent time-sensitive or priority-linked updates
- Briefing team members on their particular responsibilities and deadlines
- Announcing status review or training or any meeting arrangements
- Capturing decisions and setting out next-step action for participants.

As memos are management tools they need to be written in a business-like way, as with other documents of record. They are not conversation pieces. Points are made briefly using simple language to aid understanding. Thought must also be given to the confidentiality aspect. The views and actions are private for internal consumption only. Care must be taken with content and memos are written records and may be referred to at a later date. It is best to write and then give time to revise or delete content before circulating. Taking a break before sending allows for time to check grammar and spelling and the accuracy of statements within the memo. Pay particular attention to getting numbers, dates and names correct. I've found that it's things that are left out that are the problem. It's what's forgotten or missed out for any reason that causes the grief.

Ideally, memos should be short and to the point. As we all know, any form of written communication can be misunderstood. It is a good idea to talk about the aims and proposed content of a memo before it is sent and to include a note that if any item in the memo is unclear for any reason to make contact by phone or arrange a quick get-together to make sure everyone knows what is wanted.

Here's a memo template with notes in italics. The body text of memos is written as separate paragraphs; for the purpose of this template you will see the main text area divided by sub-headings to suggest a structural flow to your writing.

MEMO

Date: 22nd June 20XX
From: Project Manager
To: All Project Team Members (*state names or initials if a small group*)
Cc: MD of Company
Subject: Project X Status Meeting

(Paragraph 1 – State purpose of the memo)
This memo is to confirm the date, time and agenda of our next Project X Status Meeting. The meeting will be held in the small boardroom at 10.30am to 12.30pm on 25th June 20XX.

(Paragraph 2 – Main body text)
The items on the agenda with responsibility areas are:
1. Meeting opening and project overall progress assessment – SB (*names or initials of person*)
2. Critical timings statement – JW
3. Issues – TJ
4. Action Plan – HR
5. Next Steps – BS
6. Meeting close – SB

(Paragraph 3 – Reminders or requests for individuals)
Please can TJ meet me to run through the current issues and opportunities. Email me to arrange.
Can JW produce the critical timings by 24th June? Call me to confirm progress.

(Paragraph 4 – Sign-off and contact details)
We still have a long way to go to achieve our goals but your commitment and skills will, I am sure, make this project a winner.

Many thanks.

Meeting Minutes

The taking of accurate minutes of meetings is an important tool in minimising the chance of any kind of misunderstanding happening in a commercial situation, or even if you're recording decisions taken at a local flower-arranging meeting or village cricket club.

Minutes are designed to record group decisions, usually for meetings held on a regular basis with a similar core membership. They produce an evolving and continuing picture in the life of the business, club or organisation. One set of minutes sets the scene for the next and so on. Minutes log the essential information conducted at each meeting. Minutes are NOT transcripts in which every event or discussion is exhaustively covered. Minutes are an aid to memory. They create a written and agreed reminder of what took place, what decisions were taken and what actions were agreed. They clarify confusion and often settle disagreements. Having a set of minutes to refer to keeps everyone involved up to date and provides a briefing document for those who could not attend a particular meeting.

If you need to follow meeting procedure at the highest level an established authority from the UK Parliament is 'The Robert's Rules of Order', which outline a fixed order of business. However, for our purposes we will concentrate on the more flexible structures that are more likely to suit your needs.

The secret of recording accurate meeting minutes is to prepare in advance. There's a template below that will help you add elements you expect to see at the meeting. By knowing the agenda beforehand you can include items in their proposed running order and back-track to the last set of minutes to check on developments and action points that need to be updated. Meeting preparation could also include getting a list of attendees. By completing the template you will have an idea of what is going on while you are making notes. It is difficult to do the job of taking notes and participate fully in the meeting.

This is why digital recording devices are used, in addition to the chosen taker of minutes, to make notes as the meeting progresses. Notes could be typed using a laptop or tablet or pen and paper. Keeping a key-point summary from any discussion may be useful as long as it is not a running commentary, is unbiased and does not personalise matters. Unless it is the normal practice you do not have to include full names in the body of the minutes. Attendees' initials should be sufficient.

These are some of the segments in your outline template:

- Date, time and place of the meeting
- Nature of the meeting – what is the meeting designed to achieve?
- Name of meeting chair person or host
- List of attendees
- Circulation list for meeting minutes
- Apologies
- Previous Minutes – notes of any alterations made after the last meeting
- This meeting's Agenda
- Action Points and Timing
- AOB – Any Other Business
- Plans for the next meeting
- Proposed date, time and venue for the next meeting
- Attachments.

Mighty Minutes

Keeping the minutes does not mean being a silent fly on the wall. The person taking the minutes is not a spectator but someone providing an important service. When the minute-taker is jotting down notes the meeting may need to pause to clarify a point or to summarise a debate and make sure facts are recorded accurately.

It's always best to write up the minutes as soon after the meeting as possible and send a copy to the meeting host for approval before they are circulated. Minutes should be working documents for the time between meetings. If action points are time-sensitive, with a given date by which to accomplish a task, then the minutes can help plot a critical path for activity before the next meeting. While they create a record of one moment in time they should be both a reminder and stimulate thought on what happens next. When the minutes are circulated, encourage those who attended the meeting or others who are involved with the business or club to respond with proactive comments.

Voting

If a proposal needs the approval of the meeting a vote is taken. The minutes require a short description of the matter – termed a motion – along with the name or initials of the person responsible for putting the motion to the meeting and usually the name of one other member who supports the proposal. The vote is often taken by a show of hands. Motions can be recorded in this way:

Motion:
David Cannon proposed to arrange a First Aid training session for employees on 31st of the month
Vote Result:
4 votes in favour – 0 votes against
Resolved: Motion carried

Here's an example of a set of minutes. Remember to number the pages and the separate segments to help locate any topic for discussion. Modify the contents to suit your purposes, add or delete items to match your requirements.

Remember:
- Don't attempt to write everything verbatim – minutes are summaries of items
- Give priority to decisions taken, action points agreed and timings approved
- Be unbiased and objective
- Avoid any personal comments
- Keep a copy of your original notes
- Gain approval of the meeting host before circulating the minutes.
- Include your contact details
- Encourage those involved in various projects to progress-check between meetings and use the minutes as working documents
- Check grammar, spelling (especially names) and punctuation.
- I've used the classic cowboy film of *High Noon* as the example.

The High Noon Club
Minutes of the Committee Meeting held at
12pm on Monday 24th September 20XX – Venue: The Don't Forsake Me Bar

Present:

Chair: Gary Cooper	Timekeeper: Carl Foreman
Club Secretary: Grace Kelly	Minutes: Fred Zimmerman

Attendees
Lloyd Bridges
Lon Chaney Jr
Katy Jurado
Circulation: All club cast members

1.0	Apologies Lee Van Cleef, who had been detained and unable to make the meeting as in custody		
2.0 2.1	Previous Minutes The previous Minutes were read, agreed and signed	Action By GC	Date 24.09.0X
3.0 3.1	Matters Arising from Previous Minutes None		
4.0 4.1	This Meeting Agenda The proposed agenda was read and agreed – copy attached to Minutes	GC	24.09.0X
5.0 5.1 5.2 5.3 5.4 5.5	Motion: To increase the Line-Dancing Training Charge Motion proposed by GC Seconded by GK Vote: 4 For – 1 Against Motion carried Cost increase to come into effect at next month	GK	24.10.0X
6.0 6.1	Treasurer's Report The report revealed that insurance costs had tripled due to unruly behaviour by rowdy club members – renewal date as shown	LB	16.10.0X
7.0 7.1 7.2 7.3	Entertainment Programme It was confirmed that a Mechanical Bull machine and a Dolly Parton look-a-like had been booked for the next event A paramedic will be engaged as a designated driver for the night The event was confirmed for Saturday 23rd October	KJ KJ	23.10.0X
8.0 8.1	Any Other Business Committee agreed to purchase DVD of the original film *3.10 to Yuma*	GC	24.10.0X
9.0 9.1	Plans for Next Meeting Agenda to be circulated prior to meeting	GC	20.10.0X
10.0 10.1	Next Committee Meeting Dates Meetings confirmed for 24.10.0X and 24-11.0X	All Members	

CHAPTER 14

WRITING PRESS RELEASES

There are news releases and there are public relations (PR) news releases. There are similarities between the two but each is designed to do a different job. And each requires a different approach by the writer.

A standard company news release can be for internal or external purposes and its primary job is to provide information to interested parties – employees, the trade, shareholders, club or group members. The job of the PR release is to gain publicity, to gain exposure. In normal trading conditions it is aimed at the media, decision makers and people or groups of influence.

If there's a problem then PR releases are important tools in crisis management. They provide content for a company website, mainstream media, the local press and for social media in all its forms, to continue an ongoing relationship with the media and the public. This is especially important in maintaining or augmenting company, brand or product values.

As with all written communications, the content and approach depends on who you're talking to. A news release for internal purposes is to a captive audience, so you have more time and a greater word count to put your message across. You are already speaking to people who are mutually interested in what you have to say. With PR releases it's a different challenge altogether.

PR releases mainly circulated to known email addresses and personal media contacts have to be sharp, incisive, attention-getting and succinct. A standard in-house news release can have a main text section of 400 words or more. A punchy PR release circulated digitally has to capture the reader within 200 words to cut through the forest of emails arriving non-stop in their inbox. The initial email has to deliver the key information in such a compelling way that the recipient either responds to the email or picks up the phone to call you.

The Hook

Really effective releases have one thing in common – they give the media a *story*. The skill is creating a strong hook. The headline is the first hook to grab the attention of the journalist. The first all-important paragraph must reinforce the headline by adding key facts that flow from the story you've outlined. Remember that the attention-grabbing headline must punch out from the email subject header in the first place. Otherwise the chances of anyone opening and reading the full PR release are slight.

Writing a PR release is an exercise in translation: the translating of what your organisation has to say into what readers want to hear. You have got to turn your information into something that is really headline news that will benefit, stimulate or involve readers. Before you issue anything to the press you need to evaluate whether what you have to say really is newsworthy and has a beneficial story to tell or whether it is better suited to be an internal news update. Check to see if your subject falls into any of these press release categories.

Types of Press Release

- **General News:** This may be some commercial achievement or business gain in home or export markets or this may announce a new CSR (Corporate Social Responsibility) initiative
- **New Product Launch:** To coincide with the release of a new or improved product or service that has demonstrable advantages over other products in the marketplace
- **Restructuring:** Changes in the way a company operates with the advantages or effects of the changes

- **Job News:** Downsizing or creating new jobs along with the appointment or dismissal of executives
- **Events or Sponsorship:** Announcements of sporting or support for good causes

Structure

When you're ready to write your release you need to decide when it can be released. Conventionally there are two options: to distribute your news for Immediate Release or to set an Embargo on the content being used in the public domain. An embargo notice would state the date and time after which the release can be made public. In business, an embargo may be applied if the release relates to matters that are time-sensitive and should not be made common knowledge until after a meeting has been held or after an event has occurred or an important announcement has been made. The embargoed release would contain the pertinent supporting information so that when the time limit has expired the journalists can complete their text for publication.

Template Elements

1. Page/Email Header: PR Agency or Company Logo + Date For Immediate Release or Embargoed until: give the date and time.
2. Headline: Attention-grapping headline stating the key breaking news facts.
3 Sub-Headline (optional): Reinforcing and adding supporting detail to the main headlin.
4. Lead or first paragraph: Delivering the Who? What? Why? When? How? Information linked to the headline and sub-head. No more than two sentences of about 25 words each sentence delivering more facts In effect, this lead paragraph provides a condensed resume of the story that is then expanded by the main body copy text.

5. Body text:
Additional paragraphs to add more to the story and provide more detail to supplement the first paragraph. This section is where you add any personal quote statements and relevant background information that adds context to the headline story and supporting statistics. This main section is sometimes closed with a call to action to get the reader to make contact for more information. When this story section is complete use the word: 'ENDS' to signify that the facts are now complete. The remaining sections 6 – 10 are there for reference purposes.

6. Boilerplate:
This is the accepted term for a section with information about the company or organisation that is the subject of the press release.

7. Source of the release:
This is where you put details of the organisation or company that is issuing the release.

8. Media Contact Information:
Of the person to speak to about the release, name, contact phone, email details of the PR Agency or media relations contact who can answer any queries.

9. Photos/Videos:
This alerts the media to the availability of high resolution pictures for publication – rather than being sent with the release itself.

10. Notes to Editors:
These may be more information about the issuing company, details about other organisations mentioned in the release Other online links may be given to provide further context or background information.

Press Release Example

This make-believe press release adds content to the template to give you a better idea of the flow of content of a real release. The word count of this release is a short 228 words designed to capture attention online, where information has to be eye-catching and quickly assimilated by the reader.

Section	Content
Headline and Subhead	Date: 02/02/20XX **Spark Cars PR** **For Immediate Release** **Electric Car Shock** **From 0 to 60mph in 3.2 Seconds – Unbelievable?**
First Paragraph: who, what, why when, how?	The electric car revolution is no longer a myth but hard fact. The new Spark 'S' Class electric car has clocked 60mph from a standing start and has an estimated range of 310 miles.
Bodycopy: More details	Unlike a conventional internal combustion engine with hundreds of moving parts, Tesla electric motors have only one moving piece: the rotor. As a result, Model X acceleration is instant, noiseless and as smooth as silk. Step on the accelerator and in as little as 3.2 seconds, Model S is travelling 60 miles per hour, without hesitation and without a drop of petrol. Model S is an evolution in automobile engineering. All this from battery power only. This is pure electric energy. The shock of the new.
Boilerplate: Company details	Spark leads the market in battery development for electric cars. Spark batteries are being fitted into many marques of electric cars produced by the several car companies.
Source of Release: Releasing Agency	Ignition PR issued this release on behalf of Spark Electric. For any further information please contact Linda Bright on Phone/Social Media Links. Photos are available upon request. Please visit sparkcars com to view a demonstration video.
Note to Editors	These figures have been independently verified. Spark Cars are a division of Spark Engineering. Comparison with other electric car performances are available from Ignition PR.

Newsletters

Whereas the PR release has a tactical value by injecting news to heighten awareness of your organisation on one-off occasions, a newsletter performs a different marketing function altogether. It is a long-term strategic tool to build relationships. People could be introduced via your website or email marketing campaigns or you can build followers on Twitter. Newsletters help to cement the relationship and demonstrate how much you value them as customers. That's the key word: value. To gain and maintain interest and involvement your contacts must feel they are getting personal attention that qualifies them to receive:

- Special offers
- Priority status
- 'Club' benefits that relate to your product or service
- Valuable news
- Useful advice
- Opportunities to meet and interact with other contacts.

You have the choice of how regularly you send out your newsletters – either in hard copy or via email or both. It may be that your target market is a select number of people who all share an interest or activity. In this situation, deliberately posting a printed newsletter may appeal to your audience. Emails are the normal vehicle but with a deluge of emails landing in your inbox: a printed form may stand out from the crowd. But whichever route you favour, the email has got to be written, designed and relevant. Mix up the presentation to make each newsletter different to keep people interested.

Importantly, the newsletter is a way to widen your database and perhaps a way to introduce new customers to your activities. A part of this may be to speak personally to a random number of newsletter recipients and interview them to tell their story and share it in your newsletter. Make them feel happy about being one of your chosen few. If you run a story, give online links for more information. In the same way that PR releases have a 'Boilerplate,' don't forget to give your contact details along with a short statement of the main idea or purpose behind your newsletter.

I've invited Jonathan Davey to contribute to this discussion as he built his business using newsletters to promote his contact network. Jon's managed 'Business in Berkshire', a business and social network across multiple social media channels. With ad hoc meetings, he's created a vibrant interaction of people within his geographical area. Jon's energy in connecting people turns strangers into colleagues into friends who together help their business interests and the interests of their local community. Over to Jon, who in his own words will share his advice about:

THE CREATION AND VALUE OF NEWSLETTERS

Jonathan L. Davey
Network Development Specialist

In the beginning

It was the start of a new year. "How am I going to get more clients for my new email creation business?" This was the thought buzzing round my brain. The year was 2002 and very few marketing managers were willing to put their proverbial head on the block and try something new. They'd much rather spend £10k on a postal mail shot than gamble £1k on this new-fangled way of communicating with potential clients.

The irony being, back in 2002, you could achieve a 50% opening rate quite easily as people were getting probably 1% of the emails they get today! Today, if you get 20% opening and a further 20% clicking on a link, you really should be patting yourself on the back for a job well done. A good opening rate shows you are building stronger relationships as your readers take the time out of their busy lives to hear what you have to say, so don't waste their time.

Tortoise and the hare

Why would you create an email newsletter if the world is full of them, why is anyone going to open yours? The best results will be achieved by allowing people to opt-in of their own accord. Purchasing a list of 10,000 people may result in 100 being interested in what you have to say, most folk on that list being irritated by yet another uninvited email landing in their inbox. Now, if the profit of what you offer far exceeds the cost of any data, the email delivery and the creation of a template then 1 in 1000 interested might be enough to justify the expense and time, but interested doesn't mean they're ready to buy right now!

Think 'tortoise and the hare', take your time and make it interesting. Rather than volume, think quality in all things, from who gets it to what they get.

How do I fix the problem?

Are the best sales people the ones that make the most noise or the ones that are most helpful? So how about you talk about how you have solved problems for others? And if you haven't started solving problems yet, comment on potential problems you've seen in the newspapers or online.

A great structure for a short story is 'What is the problem?' for paragraph one; 'Your recommendation' in paragraph two; 'The result achieved' to finish things off, creating a nice round circle of useful information that can be easily digested and, strategically, easily shared with others.

Don't overload your reader

When you first start putting newsletters together, there can be a tendency to want to include everything you can in each email. The reality is rather like a good meal. It's best not to ruin the steak by offering too many chips and too rich a sauce. Focus on having one main topic, maybe a second relevant story, but then simply list any other titles with links to the stories so that those readers with a bit more time on their hands can spend time digesting your great content. However good your email, 99% will just have time for one story, one link before their brain says, "You'd best move on, that deadline is looming, stop procrastinating."

Help your reader digest and move on

If your content is 'to die for' then having a small taste of the good stuff means that the reader will come back for more when they have the time, or at least they'll mean to! BUT, allowing them to move on quickly will ensure that when you call in real time the reader will be happy to take your call. This time should also be used efficiently for both parties; they'll not take a second call if you waffle on. Busy people are busy for a reason, they are making money for their companies, so respect this and say what you have to say and allow them the freedom to move on; if they have a few minutes, they will kick back and spend the time with you, enhancing your relationship even more.

Initially you have a third of a second to make an impact!

How many emails do we all get? Too many is the answer. So you need to make the title work for you. It needs to create some type of reaction in the reader so they at least open the email. If you've done a good job in the past, your name might be enough (I like to think so anyway!). The reality is that you need to engage them within a blink of an eye as they scan through; once opened you will have three seconds to keep them, then 30 as they think, "This appears jolly interesting, best read more… "

What makes a good subject line for your email?

This is totally dependent on who your main audience is for the newsletter. If it is of general business interest then something topical with an appropriate leaning. If the topic is serious then best stay on message but if you can add a touch of humour, do so, as 99% of subject lines will be trying too hard to sell something. By adding a light touch you add a refreshing approach.

A few minutes insight

The purpose of your email is to strengthen your relationship with the reader and I hope you hear from the above how that means valuing their time and making it easy for them to digest what you have to say. Assuming you have 30 seconds, once they have opened the email, give them the key points on the page so they can choose to click for more if they have a personal preference for detail. Don't force them to click because you want more visitors to your web page. Most will not click and so you are reducing the potential impact of your message by probably 80% by trying to be clever and force a click. Give them a few insights in the email so they don't have to click and only have to if they really want more detail; ironically, you'll probably get more clicks that way.

Summary

- Create an engaging title.
- Make the most of your next three seconds by getting to the point in your sub-title.
- Give your reader 30 seconds, 150-250 words of jolly interesting content that demonstrates an appreciation of your reader's obvious intelligence and the fact that they are busy people.

- Give them a few key points that will share the bones of the story, allowing them to move on without clicking through to your web page for the full three-minute story. Showing respect for their time will get more clicks.

CHAPTER 15

PROPOSALS AND REPORTS

1. A Business Proposal

Whatever form it takes, a business proposal generally combines a creative idea with a financial request to fund it. This means that a strong case has to be built to support the creative and financial elements to ensure they meet company, brand or product objectives and will deliver the expected return on investment (ROI) and stay within the proposed budget. Building the case calls for gathering evidence and research to construct a persuasive argument.

Writing a proposal will use all your skills of persuasion and is the discipline that brings together the approach and arguments for the three character traits we met in the first section of the book. You need to satisfy:

1. The Visionaries – who need to be excited about the concept and it's benefits
2. The Dynamos – who need to support your executional plans
3. The Questioners – who will expect you to have done your research, have thoroughly checked any compliance issues and will grill you to get convincing answers to questions that probe your plans in the minutest detail.

Your proposal needs to have a logical structure and smooth flow to build your case. Here's one example.

Preparing and Structuring a Marketing Proposal

These steps build a proposal for management approval:

1. Background – Setting the scene – What's the current market position? What's the opportunity or the issue/s the proposal will address?
2. Target Market – Defined by gender, age, social grouping – Who are you aiming at and why?
3. Objectives – What are the business aims? What are the commercial benefits?
4. Strategy – How are the objectives going to be achieved? What is your rationale for your chosen strategy? What are your reasons for your chosen activity?
5. Tactics – A description of the detailed elements of the action plan to execute the strategy and achieve the objectives
6. Budget – How have you calculated the ROI – Return on Investment?
7. Campaign Timing
8. Next steps for approvals and key action points
9. Campaign Evaluation – After the activity has taken place what was the performance against objective? What did you learn as a result? Did you undertake research among participants?

To get a better understanding of how the nine points above are presented, here is an outline to help you get the idea.

Scenario for the Promotion Example

A publishing house is strong in conventional retail and has an impressive portfolio of writers but needs to embrace the opportunity of gaining sales via the internet. The holiday period is a prime time for gift sales and the marketing department has prepared this proposal. The budget figures are purely for demonstration purposes.

Mighty Word Publishing
Marketing Proposal: An online winter campaign showing
the breakdown structure by sub-headings

1. Background

Mighty Word Publishing performs strongly in the retail sector, both within the independent sector and major retail chains.

The company has yet to exploit sales opportunities provided by the internet, particularly during the peak winter season.

2. Target Market: Primary: Female 20-60yrs Nationwide – across all socio-economic groups (see note at end of this example).

3. Objectives
1. To generate £50,000 of online sales
2. To establish an online identity for Mighty Word Publishing
3. To raise awareness of our product range

4. Strategy
The objectives will be achieved by:
I.   Designing and launching a full e-commerce website – www.mightyword.com
II. Supporting the website with both search engine optimisation (SEO) and an online marketing campaign to include email marketing to boost awareness of our titles and authors to deliver a comprehensive viral campaign
III. Supplementing points 1 and 2 with a heavyweight sales promotion campaign aimed at delivering a pre-holiday sales uplift.

5. Tactics

The campaign strategy will be executed by:

I. Creating a fully interactive multimedia website using the written and spoken word plus online video to promote our latest authors and titles

II. Maximising our online marketing through social and business networking sites – for example: LinkedIn, Twitter, Facebook and YouTube

III. Offering a 10% discount for online orders, free gift wrapping and free gift delivery service plus a money-off voucher to stimulate post-Christmas purchases.

6. Timing

A three-month promotion starting: 1st November 20XX. Closing date 31st January 20XX

7. Budget and Cost Estimate

£25,000 – Initial costs estimated at £23,000.

8. Next Steps

- Gain management input and promotion approval
- Brief specialist web design and online agencies

9. Proposal Performance Evaluation

- Measure results against expectation – units sold and financial performance
- Selective telephone feedback research to gain consumer and trade response

Supporting Evidence

To demonstrate to all interested parties to the decision-making process that you've prepared properly you could have to hand:

- Evidence to support your market analysis and identification of the opportunity and issues
- A statement of what company resources – apart from funding – you'll need to draw on

- If you're employing outside agencies for any purpose, have supporting arguments for your choice
- A full budget breakdown to show you have anticipated the all cost centres and that your estimates are realistic
- Produce an 'Executive Summary' to aid people who are not involved in your live promotion presentation. The whole document must speak for itself and be easily understood by all readers.

A Note on Target Markets

The classification of target markets using socio-economic groups is fast becoming outdated. In marketing terms it also starts at the wrong place. To explain, the system of placing people into broad groupings was originally a market research tool. The population was divided into ABCD and E groupings. The A and B groups were the professional and upper income earners of society. The C group, which most people fell into, was sub-divided in C1 and C2 and reflected average-wage earners. C1s were mainly middle-class office workers. C2s were working-class people involved in trade activities. Ds were working class and low-wage earners and Es were retired folk with fixed incomes.

The more enlightened classification is a marketing lead approach that examines those people who are likely to be interested in your product or service. The accent is on creating a product that will appeal to a distinct group of consumers and knowing that group inside out. It is about wants and desires and consumer behaviour rather than their supposed economic class. You will hear the term 'niche marketing', which accommodates the needs of particular segments of society who have similar interests and allows for a targeted, personalised approach. Apart from knowing what consumers like, you can further segment the targeting geographically and zero in to promote by region, town and street level and select the most effective channels of communication to reach them using mainstream and social media tools to make contact.

Writing Management Reports

Although reports may cover many subjects they tend to follow a common format. Company reports are written for public or internal purposes. Public reports include the Annual Reports from large corporate companies for shareholders and are reflections of how a business has performed in the last financial year. They include a review of all commercial activities including senior management or structural changes and of course the financial picture.

However, the majority of reports are management aids written for internal reference to check on the success, or otherwise, of different projects in the normal running of the business. Reports are designed to provide a succinct briefing for busy management. They normally begin with a Management Summary followed by an expansion of the key points supported by the relevant detail. The Management Summary is the last to be written but the first to be read as it will be précis of your whole report. The Management Summary is an action-centred digest that gives recommendations and provides the key points of the fuller report.

Report Structure

1. The Title Page to include:
- Subject, name of writer or writers, date and contact details.

2. Management Summary to include:
- Project background
- Project objectives
- Performance results
- Finances – budget review
- Management Recommendations.

3. Main body of the report providing more detail for each subject

4. Report Conclusion to include:
- Issues encountered
- Lessons learned
- Next step action plan.

Three types of internal reports

1. A Market or Product Evaluation Report
    This is where research is carried out to assess a business opportunity. Often a 'S.W.O.T.', which stands for: Strengths-Weaknesses-Opportunities-Threats, analysis is used to help define the issues involved.

2. Project Updates
    These are regular progress reports in which management request a latest status report on ongoing projects. This is primarily an information gathering exercise to keep management abreast of progress, issues and costs. For instance, this may involve the installation of a new IT networking system or new machinery, in short any area that impacts upon the smooth running of the company.

3. Debriefing Reports
    These reports provide a performance assessment of company activity. This could reflect upon a marketing initiative or report on the results of company meetings – either internal or external.

Writing Reports

Remember the three key words when writing reports: purpose, clarity and brevity, when writing reports. The key thing is to communicate pieces of information accurately and be to the point. Reports should be written objectively, giving the facts and with the minimum of personal opinion. As the report is for management, adopt the correct formal tone of voice and check grammar and spelling.

Carefully prepare supporting evidence. Provide clear, easy to follow figures and charts. Be careful never to assume too much knowledge on behalf of your reader. It's far better to spend a few extra lines explaining a point rather than let your reader carry on in a fog of uncertainty.

Report Writer's Template

The following report template will help you prioritise and manage the flow of the presentation whether you're writing a commercial evaluation, project update or project debrief.

See next page.

Structural Elements	Preparation Notes
1. Title Page – Report Header Project Name – Report Author's Name, Date and Contact details – phone and email	Be clear about who the report is aimed at State date of writing and give any relevant campaign/proposal dates/action-by dates
2. Management Summary	Prioritise key points and communicate concisely Lead with achievements/developments Follow with any 'issues' Give a financial statement Summarise outcomes State supporting evidence Give recommendations
3. Main body of Report Background/Introduction/Contents	Be concise with background details to set the scene
4. Report Criteria – Objectives	Provide fuller details of report aims and achievements supported by charts and data
5. Include full details and results for each element of the report	Detail issues and implications with an assessment of solutions Provide sourced evidence to quantify issues/difficulties
6. Recommendations and Financials	State recommendations and financial costs – input and output to indicate the projected net-gains Provide rationale support for your recommendations
7. Conclusions Full Action Plan with Timing Schedule and a final 'Next Steps' Summary	Prioritise key tasks by importance and urgency Produce a timing plan and key-date schedule.
8. Supporting Appendices	Include statistical evidence and cost breakdown

CHAPTER 16

BUSINESS EMAILS AND LETTERS

Emails can be a minefield. Apart from the ones that you control in the normal course of business you are deluged with masses of clever SPAM; one moment of inattention could result in an explosion of bad news, hacking and computer viruses.

The sheer quantity of emails often leads to the equivalent of fast-food responses. I mean that they are quickly read and responded to without the necessary checking and caution. How many times have your lived to regret a hastily sent email, either because you've misunderstood or misread the incoming message or perhaps because you mean to reply to one person and realise you've whizzed off a message to people you certainly **did not** want to read your outgoing message? On top of that you have good moods and bad moods and it is easy to sound angry because you're under stress or feeling unwell.

Remember that writing instead of picking up the phone is sometimes dangerous. How many times have you meant one thing that's then been misunderstood and people have taken what you've 'said' in an email the wrong way. How often does making an offhand remark or saying something that you find hilarious fall flat – especially if the person at the other end does not know you or your sense of humour. Beware of misunderstandings.

Here are some warning flags:

- Beware of putting text in capitals; you may think this provides emphasis – the recipient may think you're shouting at them.

- Cool off – never send when you are angry. Be careful about putting anything in writing so check that what you are saying will be understood in the way you intend. Being brusque with people will be seen as disrespectful.

- Don't automatically click the 'Reply All' button – if you've received a response to an email you've sent it may be for your eyes only and not to be circulated back to the rest of the address list.

- Some message systems show the first line of the text onscreen before it is opened. Make sure what you write is appropriate for your business. You could write a first line to a friend using personal language then realise it has gone to someone who will take offence.

- Avoid running too many different subjects together. Separating subjects helps understanding in this fast-moving environment. If you mix subjects in a first email, the email conversation may only relate to one of the topics later on. New subject: new email – keep it clean and easy to manage as a subject thread.

- Never send high-priority, confidential information that could be stored in a retrieval system without considering the immediate and future consequences of the contents becoming available to third parties.

- Use the appropriate language and tone of voice. Check grammar and correct any literals before sending. Once again, in the superfast world of business it is easy to send a message that looks unprofessional due to the pressure of work at the time you've sent the message.

- Don't forget to add attachments!

Other Pointers

- Emails are read quickly – so get to the point quickly and include any request for action in the first paragraph. Use simple, clear language and a good size of type that is easy to read.
- Think about the problem of repeatedly replying to a received email, adding new text to an original message. The original title may no longer reflect the evolving message content and unless you begin a fresh email the length will mean printing reams of paper when you only want to read the latest exchange.
- Give as full a description as possible in the 'Subject' section to state the purpose of the email and identify you as the sender of the email to avoid a business connection pressing the delete button thinking your email is SPAM.
- Think about the person/s you're sending it to. It's easy to get so engrossed in writing the email content that you could overlook something that is inappropriate to others on the address list.
- If the email is the first contact you have with someone, adopt a formal approach. This demonstrates respect. A more informal style can follow for further exchanges once the relationship has been established.
- In case the recipient wants to print out your email to be filed, it can help to repeat the email subject at the top of the message space along with the date of sending. Repeating the key information at the top of the main text body adds clarity and helps focus the reader's attention to aid understanding.(See example below.)
- Emails should be seen as confidential and private. A legal note should be included to that effect along with a request to delete any email that has been wrongly received.

Email Section Structure Example

Email to:	To: b.wiggins@wigginswidgets.com
Copy	cc p.nocchio@universalgizmos.com
Subject Line – Full and Complete Details description with name of sender included	Guy Gizmo – Meeting Confirmation 14th December 20XX
Message Text 1. Date sent: 2. Repeat of Email Subject: 3. Greeting (in this case informal) 4.Main Message Text	Today's date: 1st November 20XX Confirmation of Widget and Gizmo Merger Meeting 9.30am-12.00pm 14th December 20XX Dear Barnaby, A quick note to confirm our meeting at your offices on Monday 14th December at 9.30am. I will be accompanied by Peter Nocchio, Head of our Wooden Toys Division. We look forward to discussing our future plans.
5. Regards and Full Sender Contact Details to include hyperlinks to emails and websites	Best regards **Guy Gizmo** Guy Gizmo Business Development Manager – Universal Gizmos Telephone: 0800 247 247 Mobile/Cell: 07084 127 234 Email: guy@universalgizmos.com www.universal gizmos.com Follow me on Twitter Follow me on Google + Find me on LinkedIn

Confidentiality Statement	Please consider the environment before printing this email. This email may contain confidential and privileged information and is subject to copyright. If you are not the intended addressee please delete the message. Please note that any distribution, copying or use of this information is prohibited. If you have received this email in error please inform us immediately by email or telephone us on xxxxx before completely deleting the message.

This Plain Text Email demonstrates:

- How to improve the communication value of a simple email
- How to sharpen up the 'Subject' line to telegraph the importance of email content
- How to structure content to be clear and easier to understand.

1. The Subject Line

- The name of the sender is given to identify the email as coming from a known source that connects with a subject that concerns you to signal this is NOT SPAM.
- It also flags up the purpose of the email and provides in this example the important date of the meeting.
- State the topic and any action required in the subject line; this could be:
- New Logo Design – Feedback please by 7th June 20XX
- Product Launch Recommendation – Action needed by – state date
- PR Release Attached – Legal approval needed by– state date.
- If you're sending supporting information, point this up in the subject line with FYI (For Your Information) or state 'For Reference Only' or 'Download & Save' or 'Reference Only – No Action Required' for instance:
  'Steve B –Transform Your Communication Skills – First Draft FYI'.

2. The Main Body Text

- Reprise the date and purpose of the email at the top of the message section to reinforce the reason for sending. This is also helpful when printing out a hard copy for filing reference or to use as handouts at a meeting. This new idea looks professional and helps reinforce the role of the particular email.
- The simple email below is written as Plain Text that does not allow any bullet points or numbering using M/S Word.
- To insert bullet points or numbering go to the top tag of Format Text – then select either HTML or Rich Text as shown in the second example below.
- Supply full contact details so you can be easily contacted; you may wish to include social media, Twitter, LinkedIn and Facebook details.
- If you're reacting to a request for information it helps to highlight this aspect in the subject line. You can identify yourself as the sender to give the recipient confidence that the email should be virus free, that's assuming you are communicating with people you know. For instance: 'Your name – Brand Presentation Request – Document Attached'.

3. Confidentiality Statement

Confidentiality statements are disclaimers in case emails get into unintended hands. They are normally added by organisations that want to limit any damage caused by information going astray.

Here's one that covers these three key elements:

1. Statement relating to the confidential nature of the information contained in the email
2. Virus message to show that steps have been taken to avoid the email carrying any contamination
3. An alert to stress that emails as a medium are not totally secure.

Disclaimer

Confidentiality: This email transmission is strictly confidential and intended solely for the addressee. It may contain privileged and confidential information and if you are not the intended recipient, you must not copy or distribute it. If you have received this email in error, please notify the sender and delete the email transmission immediately.

Viruses: Although we have taken steps to ensure that this email and attachments are free from any virus, we advise that in keeping with good computing practice, the recipient should ensure they are actually virus free.

Security Warning: Please note that this email has been created in the knowledge that internet email is not a 100% secure communications medium. We advise that you understand this lack of security and take any necessary measures when emailing us.

HTML or Rich Text Example

An HTML or Rich Text format allows you to include bullet points and numbering to help lift and separate the content. Here is a before and after example of the impact on a solid text. Notice that, as well as the addition of numbering and bullet points, the sub-headlines are now in bold to help the flow of information.

Original Message to be sent to client:	Revised Text with Bullet Points and Number Formatting
Subject: Promotional Plan	Subject: SPB – Promotional Plan – Presentation date 12th August xxxx – Creative Development Outline
Hi! Lindsay, I thought it would be helpful to describe the steps we are going take to develop the new spring promotion. The account team will meet to discuss your brief and confirm the promotion objectives. Concepts will be created and scrutinised until we have at least three options for you to consider. The favoured options will then be given to our studio for them to create presentation visuals. The shortlisted concepts will be presented internally to senior management. Each concept will then be written up and a cost estimate will be produced. Importantly, each one will be thoroughly researched to ensure all elements can be executed on time and on budget. If you have any questions please get in touch.	Hi! Lindsay, In advance of our promotion presentation date of the 12th August XXX I thought it would be helpful to outline the creative process we adopt internally to develop concepts for our clients. **These are the steps we take:** 1. The Account Team meet to discuss your brief and confirm the promotional objectives 2. Concepts will be created and scrutinised until we have at least three options for you to consider 3. The shortlisted concepts will be given to our studio to create presentation visuals 4. The shortlisted concepts will be presented internally for senior management approval. **Each concept will be:** • Written up with full details • Provided with a cost estimate • Fully researched • Checked to make sure all elements can be executed on time and on budget. If you have any questions please get in touch.
Best regards Mike Smithers Account Director Promo Solutions Inc. *(full contact details printed here)*	Best regards Mike Smithers Account Director Promo Solutions Inc. *(full contact details printed here)*

Writing Business Letters

It's true that the heyday of business letter writing is long gone, with the majority of B2B communications taking place over the net with the advent of email, Skype, video, SMS text and other forms of digital platforms.

But there are many occasions where letter-writing skills are still needed, for example letters of complaint, 'thank-you' letters, letters for accepting a job offer or letters of resignation. The more difficult to write are well-judged cover letters and letters of introduction to a new business prospect. Here are some suggestions to help your letter get noticed and put onto the desk of the person you want to contact. Many letters are screened and placed in the bin before the letter is even fully unfolded. These suggestions will improve your chances of success.

1. Letters of Introduction

Writing effective contact letters will gain business. In an email-dominated world of cyber static, the incisive use of a carefully researched, accurately targeted, well-constructed letter has a good chance of getting noticed, especially if the purpose and benefits of the letter are clear and compelling. Also, by writing a letter you are doing something unexpected. And if you do the unexpected well, with style and class, then you may just get the break you hope for.

How to increase your chances of success

- Use a carefully targeted approach when writing to new business prospects. Go for quality rather than quantity and tailor your message to a selection of chosen targets so that you can develop a more personalised introduction.
- Do your research — find out about your target company, their market, their competitors and their issues.

- Identify the correct person to contact – name, title, business responsibilities. Try to gain extra insight into the character of the person you're contacting. Your target may have a business or social networking page. Check them out.
- Don't assume the most senior person is the right person for that important first approach – find out who has the influence, it may be someone a tier lower than you'd expect.
- Develop a proposal to generate business for your prospect – what benefit/s can you bring to the table?
- Think creatively about the nature of your communication – what will make you stand out in the morning mail?
- Don't combine an introduction with a full-on sales pitch – take one step at a time and get the balance of the message right.
- Use the letter as the opening gambit, as a means to gain a meeting or advance your cause in a positive way.
- Always follow-up, via phone or email; don't be nervous about making the first move. Accept failure as the price for achieving success – keep going.

Yours Faithfully or Yours Sincerely: What is the correct way of topping and tailing a letter?

If you are writing to someone you do not know, for example a 'Dear Sir or Madam' letter the sign-off term is 'Yours Faithfully'.

If you've identified a person, for example: 'Dear Mr Wiggins' or someone you know well enough to use their forename, the sign off term is 'Yours Sincerely'.

Example of a Letter of Introduction

Notice the text below delivers the message crisply on a single page of A4. The letter opens with the main point of arranging a meeting, goes on to explain the benefits, then closes with proposed action as follows:

To:
Barnaby Wiggins
Business Development Manager – Wiggins Widgets
Widget House etc…

Widgets and Gizmos Alliance Proposal

Dear Mr Wiggins,

I'm writing to introduce my company, Universal Gizmos, and to request a meeting. The aim will be to explore an alliance between our two companies for mutual benefit.

Wiggins Widgets has particular strengths in the design and marketing of innovative products for the children's market. Universal Gizmos has built a strong reputation for their range of products aimed at adults and has a new production facility. An alliance would help us to break new ground in sales and marketing both at home and abroad with a united strategy.

I believe there's a natural synergy between the quality and imagination of both our product ranges. I enclose our latest spring brochure and look forward to discussing the opportunities that lie ahead.

I will telephone you shortly to compare diaries and arrange a meeting. If you'd like to get in touch as a result of this letter, I can be reached on 0707 123 456.

I look forward to meeting you,
Yours sincerely,
Guy Gizmo
Business Development Manager – Universal Gizmos

Summary of Letter Key Points

• Guy had researched Barnaby's name and title in order to speak to his correct opposite number – and, having identified a person, he signed off using 'Yours sincerely'.

- Guy used just two sentences to establish who was writing and what he wanted. The closing lines repeat the request and action to be taken to arrange a meeting.
- Guy immediately talks about the benefits of a commercial alliance.
- By explaining his position simply and clearly, Guy added a clear purpose and improved his chances of being taken seriously.
- Guy was not trying to sell anything. He demonstrated his positive intentions by including the spring brochure for information.
- Notice that the last few sentences are not run together in paragraph form. They have been written as separate statements to add emphasis. The added benefit of separating these last lines makes your contact details easier to find and act upon by the recipient.

2. Non-CV Cover Letters – Don't miss an opportunity

Hard copies of important reports, agreements and documents are sent to clients for their attention. Often a cover letter is included out of courtesy and added as an after-thought in the belief the document contains all that is required. This is an opportunity missed.

A cover letter can:

- Be a key-point reminder of content of the enclosed document
- Outline the benefits and reinforce the enclosed proposition
- Repeat details of a project timeline and a key-date schedule for any decision making
- Strengthen any personal relationship by developing trust and commitment to a project
- Recap on a conversation related to the business in hand.

3. CV Cover Letters – Please fast forward to the end of Chapter 19, which deals with writing CVs, Resumes and One-Pagers and has template guides for each option.

CHAPTER 17

WRITING A BUSINESS CASE STUDY
REPUTATION MARKETING

Case studies are business stories

Case studies reflect the kind of organisation you are, the kind of people you are and the kind of approach you adopt to help your client's business flourish. The use of language, the style of writing, the variety of topics covered and importantly, the successful results you helped to create, speak volumes.

Put simply, case studies are business stories that contain three sections: a beginning, a middle and an end under the general content headings of:

1. The Challenge
2. Your Solution
3. The Gains.

Remember that case studies to be posted online are shorter in word count, more direct and get to the point faster than ones used in brochures or other forms of offline media.

Tone of Voice

Writing a business study is evidential marketing. Essentially it is a collaborative venture between client and agency. As such, the tone should be professional, supportive and respectful – and approved before release. Case studies are credential statements that are part of the overall marketing mix to raise awareness and gain new business by demonstrating the quality of expertise that has benefitted your past and existing clients. Be aware that you should provide enough information without giving too much away.

Writing Tips

Assemble your raw material. Sort it into the three core sections. Then write for the reader.

1. Begin with a bold headline to capture the key end-benefit for your client.
2. Provide a supporting sub-heading sentence that reinforces the achievement stated in the headline.
3. Use sub-headings to punctuate the piece and underline the essence of the related paragraph.
4. 'Pull Out' using text boxes, images or charts from the surrounding text to highlight quotes, testimonials, statistics and relevant pictures (avoid hackneyed photo library shots).
5. Avoid jargon and acronyms – or if you have to use them, explain what they mean in layman's language.
6. Use short sentences and short paragraphs. Keep the word-use simple for maximum comprehension.
7. Review and update to see how your input has continued to benefit a client over time.

If you're writing a marketing case study, this structure is frequently adopted: Headline – Background – Objective – Strategy – Implementation – Results

If the marketing case study is written for internal use an extra section is often added: Next Steps or Lessons Learned. This section highlights aspects that need to be addressed and improved upon or operational issues that either worked well or malfunctioned.

Market Your Case Studies:

- On your website
- On any separate BLOG/VLOG site
- Post keywords and phrases on Wordpress SEO support sections
- In a podcast – include a client contribution, maybe arecorded interview
- In a video version, ideally with client involvement, on your website and YouTube account; produce a short URL link to send to any prospective client
- By using them as PR releases with your URL address and contact details.

BUSINESS CASE STUDY – A WRITER'S TEMPLATE

Case studies have a beginning, middle and end.

They are part of your reputational marketing programme. They:

- Showcase your skills
- Reinforce Your Credentials
- Promote Your Capabilities
-

Importantly you must provide clear evidence of success.

Each case study can be written in three lengths depending on where they'll be posted: short for online, medium for blogging, and long for printed brochures and magazine articles. Here is a guide to the word count for each section.

1. Short: 300 words	2. Medium: 500 words	3. Long: 750 Words
For online posting: 150/200 words max	For online posting (blogging) 500 words should be the longest	For corporate brochures or magazine articles
Word Count Guide	Word Count	Word Count
Beginning: 50	Beginning: 100	Beginning: 150
Middle:200	Middle: 300	Middle: 450
End: 50	End: 100	End: 150

Content Structure

BEGINNING			MIDDLE	END	
Set the Scene	The Challenge	Your Capabilities Why You?	Your Solution What you Recommended	Results	Benefits
Client Profile Describe the business situation	The Pain Point Describe the problem the client faced	What special skills or experience did you have to solve the problem	Your approach: reasoning, techniques, implementation, process, timing	Statistical evidence/ proof charts/ photos	Client Gains/ Savings Client Testimonials

Case Study Example from Steve Preston MD of SMP Solutions

An introduction to the SMP Solutions case study

SMP Solutions are a career – and people – development consultancy working with businesses and private clients. SMP Solutions are creators of the unique 'Six-Step Change Cycle'. This highly effective tool can be personalised and applied to Career Transition, Business Performance Improvement and Personal Coaching Projects.

This case study concerns an executive outplacement project. To explain, executive outplacement is when career transition support and advice is sought by someone who needs to reassess their career direction and plan for the future, as a result of redundancy or a compromise agreement with their employer.

The SMP Six-Step Career Navigation Cycle process is designed to help people:

- Manage the emotional reactions to change
- Let go and move forward with confidence
- Re-evaluate their career and life goals
- Establish skills, attributes, hidden talents and true marketability
- Work through career and life options
- Focus, gain clarity and discover a new direction
- Unlock and fulfil potential to achieve a new career and life path
- Take positive action to achieve their goals.

Explanation of Writing Terms used below:

1. Headline and Strapline or Crosshead (a crosshead is another term for 'strapline'): A headline with a supporting subsection printed as an integral part of the headline statement.
2. Pull-Out: Either a photo, image or supporting information or testimonial that is set within the body of the text to add interest and catch attention.
3. Subhead: A short text heading to flag up a new thought or idea and alert the reader that a fresh important points is about to be made.
4. In the real-life example below the content elements are highlighted using italics.

Case Study Example:

Headline and Subhead:

SMP Solutions Executive Outplacement Relights a Fire: Senior Executive Reinvents Herself to Power Forward

Beginning section: Scene setting and identifying the challenge – the pain point

After twenty-eight years of corporate service, the time had come for a senior executive to leave her employment. She doubted her capabilities without the corporate umbrella and had no clear idea what the future would hold. She had learnt many management techniques but when it came to applying them to herself she needed outside help. She wanted an organisation that would not adopt a 'one size fits all' solution but would support and guide her on a personal level. It was important to work with people with a track record of success who would have the right professional chemistry to coach and support her during this massive challenge of change.

Word count for this section: 111

Middle section: The SMP approach – the solution

Contact was made by the senior executive with the MD Steve Preston via LinkedIn. The SMP Managing Director, Steve Preston, listened to the fears and tangled weeds of concerns that had built up in the executive's mind. Steve began to turn those fears into focus, which quickly lessened anxiety. The skills of two further members of the SMP team came into play. One added weight to help her create a new personal brand that harmonised all the executive's talents and attributes into one impressive identity. Another undertook coaching to sharpen high-level presentation and pitching skills.

Word count of this section: 96
End Section: The results and benefits gained

Over the next few months the use of the SMP Six-Step Career Navigation Cycle with other dedicated tools and techniques revitalised dormant passions and optimism. The result was that the executive had relit the fires of enthusiasm. She now had the courage to leave her old employer to create her own business in a field that she loved. The overall combination of executive outplacement toolkit and personalised, targeted support produced the desired result. Not only was a new career direction clearly defined but the positive vibes rippled down to the friends and family who witnessed a re-energised person relishing the prospect of a new and fulfilling future.

Pull-out of client testimonial:

"Steve and his team have turned my dark world into a glorious bright future — and I'm sure he can do the same for you. Don't delay. Turn your fear into focus and take charge of your own future."
Jane S. Buckinghamshire.
End section word count: 148

Total word count for case study: 355

CHAPTER 18

WRITING A BUSINESS PLAN

Presenting a business idea

There's a chance that your existing business may want to update their business plan and you may become involved. Or you may be thinking of setting up your own business and you'll need to know how to write your first plan. Learning the basics of writing a business plan and knowing what potential investors are looking for to encourage them to put money into your business will be a great help.

Writing a business plan is an exercise that:

- Is important to prove to yourself that the concept is commercially viable
- Will demonstrate to family and friends that your business venture is sound enough to gain their support. Family support is a vital factor to provide emotional and perhaps financial support
- Will provide hard evidence to the bank or to business investors that you have a potential winner.

A business plan needs to cover these essential elements:

- An introduction that describes the business model, including its aims and the structure of the organisation, its legal entity, trading operation and key personnel

- The business model's brands, products, marketing and sales practices
- The financial picture. This may be a statement of the current performance if already trading or a proposed financing plan if a new business start-up
- A growth forecast to include marketing, product or brand development and estimated financial investment and returns.

Business Model Planner

Here are points to remember when preparing a first business plan:

1. Demonstrate both an understanding of the immediate task of launching the business and the need for steady management over the short term.
2. The business plan should present the short term, the next 12-18 months and if possible an indication of growth for the first three years.
3. Describe your vision of the future potential and scope for development. Is the business scalable, i.e. can it be expanded into a national or international business?
4. Remember to play 'Devil's Advocate' and question your own assumptions. Be prepared for probing questions from banks or other investors or lenders.
5. Use the SMART acronym to help set and describe your business goals:

    S = Specific – set accurate targets to achieve

    M = Measurable – use bookkeeping or sales techniques to provide evidence of how successful you are being in reaching your specific targets

    A = Achievable/attainable – base your targets on what is realistic in the current circumstances; business takes time to grow and you need to make allowances for a changing commercial environment

    R = Relevant – goals should be based on what is rooted in real and known commercial situations

    T = Time-related – try to set goals that can be achieved within a practical and manageable time frame. Relate the goal with time e.g. to increase sales by 10% in six months.

Business Plan Writing Sequence

The management summary is the last section you write but the *first* people will see. It is vital to make an impressive first impression. Take care to create a confident, realistic, financially sound, well-researched management summary.

Section Sequence	Content Suggestions
Front Page	Your business name – document dedicated to a person, organisation or investor with your contact details and date of presentation
Management Summary	Essentially stating the Commercial Viability of the concept – Business proposition, description of the nature of the business – Business sector, mode of sales/service operation – Legal entity – Key personnel – Financial profile – Start-Up investment needed – Commercial research and competitors – Launch date
Business/Sales Strategy	Description of commercial operation – Routes to market – Particulars on business set-up requirements – Business objectives and operational goals – Business sustainability –Growth forecast in detail for first 12 months – Any commercial alliances
Marketing Strategy	Creation of business name, Trade Marking, Website domain name, site design and email, Brand/Product logo design, packaging and presentation, Launch promotional strategy
Management Structure	Roles and relevant skills of key personnel, Employed/self-employed status, Supporting administrative roles, Appointment of advisors, Accountants, Legal, Business, Marketing
Finance Forecasts and Budgets	Capital set-up costs, Forecast Income and Expenditure, On-going fixed costs and anticipated variable costs, Budget for Working Capital, Sales Forecast, Cash Flow Forecast, Break-Even, Profit and Loss Forecast – All providing evidence of the commercial viability of the business concept to include personal survival fund
Supporting Appendices	Examples of progress made in the pre-start-up period – logo designs, product or packaging information – competitive information and assessments

12 points to impress investors

When writing it's a good idea to imagine how the piece you're working on will be received. These 12 points will set the bar of achievement. If you produce a piece that will tick these boxes then you've done a great job. We'll start with some general points for a version of your business plan to be presented either to your bank or potential investors.

The management summary should be no longer than two pages. To recap, the job of the summary is to give an overview of your business plans and communicate the key points, but leave the detail to the supporting sections. The tone, and to some extent the content, will vary depending on who you're writing for.

If you have all the finances in place and the business plan is primarily for your management purposes then your first business plan will provide the benchmark for future achievements.

If, on the other hand, you're writing to attract a potential investor or for a bank manager, the aim is to make them:

1. Excited by the idea and your ability to make it work
2. Impressed with your depth of knowledge of the market and the competition
3. Confident of your personal business background and management talent
4. Reassured of your people-management skills
5. In agreement with your financial assessment and the method you've used to calculate the future business prospects
6. Stimulated by your marketing ideas and sales support strategy
7. Greatly encouraged by your cash-flow management plans and profit forecast
8. Approving of the amount of money you're asking for and what you intend to spend it on

9. Supportive of your projections that will lead to an exit strategy for the investor
10. Appreciative of the personal investment you are contributing as your stake in the business
11. For an investor, accepting of the percentage share in the business you have proposed in return for the financial backing
12. Thrilled if you can prove your idea is scalable – to be increased in size when proven successful.

If you're writing to get a bank loan, then the emphasis should be placed on the strength of the business concept and your ability to generate a sufficient commercial profit. Expect any lender to ask for personal guarantees for any money lent to you and to ask for another person of substance to act as your guarantor – normally a member of your family.

The First but not Last Business Plan

Writing a business plan will give you confidence that you're on the right track. Your business plan will reflect one moment in time, the time it was written. The first plan is immensely valuable but should be refined and updated by events. Don't stick to it like glue. Improve and develop the plan as circumstances change. Continue to build on the strong foundations you've created.

CHAPTER 19

CVS, RESUMES AND ONE-PAGERS
BE OUTSTANDING!

You've come far and increased your range of talents. It follows that at some point you will seek pastures new. Everyone has their own story. Everyone is at a different stage in their working life. By practising the skills covered in these pages you will stand out and flourish. Preparing the best representation of your talents will take you where you want to go.

New technology and the growth in social media are overturning the norms that once dictated the way people apply for jobs in terms of content and techniques used to attract attention. Here are three descriptions and guidance templates for a classic CV, a career resume and a one-page approach. What's the difference?

Non-Digital CV – Curriculum Vitae: Latin for 'Course of Life'

A conventional CV encapsulates key facts about you and your current and past employment situations. In addition to your employment history it records your educational and professional achievements and achievements in your private life, like sporting awards for instance. It touches on personal interests but the focus is very much on your work experience. A CV typically runs to between two to three pages. Increasingly, personal profiles are written to provide more detail on your current position and skills. A CV is written in reverse chronological order, beginning with the most up-to-date information then working backwards to cover the place, time and job where you started. Employers will ask questions if there is a time gap between employers. Importantly, a traditional CV is very much a reference document, but you can add a profile section that addresses your suitability for a particular job opportunity. More information about your skills and ability is contained in the CV cover letter.

Depending on the nature of the employer and the business market they occupy, you have to judge whether to include a head-and-shoulders business photograph of yourself. Despite the massive impact of social media, where the posting of photos is an accepted practice, there are organisations that will not accept CV photographs of job applicants for fear of being accused of discrimination on the grounds of gender and race. Check with the employment agency or direct with the employer on their policy. You will find that CV usage changes by country. Some traditionally favour the standard CV, such as the UK. There is a European Union format that does require a passport photo and details of citizenship, marital status and children. In the USA a resume is the accepted format for job applications.

Use this layout as a template guide for a written CV of someone who has a track record and previous work experience. The flow of information categories can be adjusted to suit your story. In this example we are leading with Melissa's work experience and aptitude for a more senior marketing position.

If you are just starting out you would still write a short but interesting profile and then support it with your education and any relevant work experience. It is important if just starting out to provide information on what your interests are and any volunteer or community involvement you have had, along with sporting or leisure activities that help to paint a picture of the type of character you are.

The text in italics suggests the kind of information to include under each sub-heading. Change the heading order to suit your needs. If you are including a fuller personal profile statement the first five would probably remain in the same sequence. Keep your CV updated as your career develops.

Melissa Young

(You can add links to social media if business-related)

Telephone: 0201 324 4356 Mobile/Cell 07943 121 231 – Email: my@home.me

14 The Beeches, Old Musings, Somewhere or Other TD1 7BS

Profile

(A statement supporting your suitability for a particular job, researched and tailored for the purpose)

Current Position: Marketing Executive Competitive Company

My experience over the years, the achievement levels, consistent performance and being an able Team Leader has prepared me for the position of marketing manager with Mega Marketing Inc.

Areas of Expertise

(Your expertise prioritised in order of relevance to the position you're going for)

Client Communications, Computer Literate, Campaign Strategy, Copywriting, Client Presentations, Team Leader, Brand Management

---

Professional Qualifications

(Evidence of continued learning and development post-university, college or school)

Diploma in Advertising, Higher Certificate in Marketing, Diploma in Direct Marketing

---

Employment Record

(Details of employer, roles and achievements while with them)

20XX to date: Competitive Company

- Developed marketing strategy for 2009 online sales campaign
- Briefed creative team on Award Winning radio campaign
- Provided copywriting support for campaign team

20XX – 20XX: Graduate Trainee with Another Competitive Company

- Learned how to operate Apple Quark
- Provided client support for national retail promotion
- Joined the top performing Account Team

Work Experience
(To include internships and voluntary work)
20XX-20XX: Unpaid internship at Radio Ga Ga
20XX – 20XX: Six-month work experience with Women's Magazine at University
20XX – 20XX: Editor of University Magazine
20XX – 20XX: Community Volunteer for Care Homes – visiting the aged

Education
(Include subject breakdown and grade achievement if a first CV)
20XX – 20XX University of Wisdom Graduated with BA Honours in Business Communications
20XX – 20XX College gaining 3 'A' Levels and 10 GCSE 'O' Levels

Interests and Awards
(The more varied the better, or achievement in one area to give an idea of the kind of person you are)
Martial Arts
• Black belt Ju Jitsu
Performing Arts
• Member of local Amateur Dramatic Society Sports
• Captain of the School Hockey Team Writing
• Blogger and writer of short stories

References
(To stop referees being inundated with requests you may state: 'References are available upon request' or provide more information such as: 'Referee contact details will be supplied')
• Competitive Company Inc. My previous employer
• Another competitive company. Employer from 20XX – 20XX
• Radio Ga Ga

Online CVs and VCVs

It is inevitable that digital forms of communication will alter the shape of communication dramatically. Online CVs using slide-sharing software such as Slideshare and Prezi will be the option for some and video CVs for others.

There will be stepping-stone options too, where conventional written CVs or resumes are required on their own or appended to a digital format. As with earlier advice, check with the employer to see if an online CV is required or optional. It is more likely in sales, marketing, performing arts or new media than in the conventional professions of the law or accountancy. However, it is the quality of the production and relevance of the message and general creativity that may determine whether you get the interview.

Also, if you choose the online route the nature of the whole presentation moves from a written record of employment and achievement to an online performance using slide share or video. The presentation would be geared to showing you in the best light as well as pitching for a particular job. Clearly this would favour people who are gregarious and extrovert – that's unless you pay good money to produce a professional video. If you do opt for a VCV keep it short (no more than 90 seconds), as recruiters are not likely to sit through a 2-3-minute presentation unless you are super-talented and are already on the shortlist. The reality of using a VCV is that the recruitment world may not be ready for it as it could be a nightmare of litigation if decisions from viewing a video contravene the discrimination guidelines.

At the time of writing I would suggest that a multimedia CV with a combination of slides, music and images, cleverly contrived, with an inventive message treatment appropriate for the end-user and supported by the attachment of a conventional CV could be an answer.

Resume vs. CV

A resume in the UK is a strategic, concise, highly targeted document. It is designed to get you on the consideration shortlist by focussing on your aptitude, experience and suitability for a particular job specification. A resume is written afresh for each job application to realign your talents and skills to meet the requirements of each opportunity. The resume does not have to be chronological and it does not have to cover every aspect of your past experience – just the aspects that will win the day. As such, resumes are typically one page long and written to be digested quickly by the recruiter. Due to the nature of resumes, they are used by people who already have a track record of experience and professional achievement.

This is an example of a resume template.

John Egan Resume
Telephone xxxxx Mobile/Cell xxxxxxxx Email: john@egan.me
(LinkedIn logo)
Objective
(State the position you are seeking)
Application for the position of Creative Director of Mega Marketing Designs Inc.
Profile Summary
(A pen portrait of your talents and suitability for the positon – stressing the contribution you will make)
I have a rare combination of creative and commercial abilities. My contribution to Mega Marketing would span the creative genres, as evidenced by the recognition and awards plus the way my team leadership has added real growth to the financial bottom line.
Experience and Accomplishments
(Details of current and past employment, awards gained and key accomplishments)
Job Title – Company Name – City – Dates
•   Winner of the 20XX Design of the Year •   Winner of the 20XX Best Campaign
Skills
(State the range of skills starting with the ones most appropriate for the job)
•   Digital Design and Marketing •   Online Design and Marketing •   Team Leadership •   Commercial Training

Professional Qualifications, Education and References
(Focus on professional and further education achievements)
Diploma in Design
MA in Creative Design
References available upon request

Activities
(List personal achievements and involvements)
Sporting achievements, extracurricular involvements, personal interests

One-Pagers: A Fresh Approach to Job Applications

There's a new approach to job applications that has a completely new take on resumes. The key difference is that conventional CVs and resumes record who you are and what you've done. They look at you through the rear-view mirror. The new resumes are concerned not so much with what you've done but with what you're capable of doing in the future. They are an indication of your potential. Of course, past performance is featured but the past is not taken as a guide to future attainment.

While normal resumes are aimed at a wider job market, a one-pager is written only for one organisation, one position and the one identified reader of the proposal. In order to get considered for a position the applicant is given a particular brief to answer. Either that or they adopt a one-page approach and take the initiative to identify an issue to be solved or an opportunity to be exploited. In this way they would display their skills, their problem-solving ability and produce a 'live' demonstration of the contribution they would make in real time for an actual project. A one-page approach could have fuller personal details in a conventional resume appended to your recommendation. The two together will reinforce your desire to work for and show commitment to your new employer.

The one-pager will capture the key steps you've taken to:

- Research the market
- Identify the problem (the pain) or the opportunity (the gain)
- Propose a solution
- Calculate the 'upside' benefits in marketing and commercial terms
- Impress the recruiter with the razor-sharp thinking and clear, concise presentation of the concept.

This is a rough one-pager outline template to give you an idea of how to proceed. The process is to do all the preparation and research before you identify a valuable opportunity (not just an opportunity but one that will make money). Then reveal your recommendation, working back from the brief to your solution and supporting evidence.

Your Contact Details
Position Applied For
Objective *(Outline the problem or opportunity)*
Strategy *(State the steps to take to solve the problem/exploit the opportunity)*
Rationale *(Explain your approach – research – analysis – identification – evidence – solution*
Results *(Estimated gains – Return on Investment – Brand share – Sales – Distribution)*
Personal Profile *(Describe your suitability for this position and what this one-pager has demonstrated as your potential)*
Professional Qualifications, Education, Accomplishments *(Bullet points only)*

CV Cover Letter – Writing a CV/Resume/One-Pager Cover Letter
(Please revisit the general letter writing tips in Chapter 14.)

When using a conventional CV, the cover letter or cover email is vital to provide further information about you and the reasons for applying for a role.

Yes, the profile section in a CV or resume also provides space too for this purpose but a well-crafted covering note could be the ticket to an interview as it can reveal a great deal to a potential recruiter. The structure and discipline, the choice of language, the persuasiveness of the content, whether hand-written or typed, are all strong signals encoded in a page or half a page.

The cover letter is the place to argue your case. Depending on the nature of the job, you need to think about the most appropriate approach to make your talent shine through. This is the opportunity to explain why you want to work for the employer, what makes you best suited to fulfil the job specification and what positive contribution you can make to their commercial performance. As with the one-pager, the cover letter is where you concentrate on what the employer's issues are and how you can make a difference.

Avoid stringing out a list of overused adjectives that are CV wallpaper, for instance:

- Good team player
- Hard working
- Highly motivated.
- Concentrate more on the tangible, proven and valuable talents such as:
- Communication skills that span speaking, writing and presenting at all levels
- Proven mediation skills
- Problem-solving experience gaining positive outcomes
- Commitment to supporting trade shows and exhibitions
- Voluntary involvement in brain-storming sessions
- Leadership skills
- Language skills
- Training and skill development of colleagues.

If you've gone through a process of thorough preparation you may have identified an area where you feel that you can make an impact. Point this up to highlight and provide proof that you will be an asset, to show you are already thinking as if you're a part of their team, someone who understands and wants to be a part of their culture. When it comes to the interview stage, be pro-active and interview them on issues that demonstrate you are on their wavelength. But I'm getting ahead of myself. I'd better get back to writing the letter.

Recruiters can take seconds to reject or retain applications. When so many A4 sheets of paper or emails vie for their attention it is the ones that literally 'speak their language' that they notice. Recruiters expect to see the submissions that fall into the same predictable groove; it's the ones that not only tick the expected boxes but that fly above the flock of the ordinary to be extraordinary that they will remember.

Positive, confident use of language will drive you forward. Make your points using active words that indicate pace and dynamism. Active words generate energy to lift your words off the page and catch the attention. Words like these and statements like these:

- I *evaluated* the opportunity and *managed* the development and *execution* of the project
- *Together* my team *devised* and *achieved* a *breakthrough* in the market
- I *led* a team that *negotiated* special rates that *achieved* our quarterly targets in *record* time.

Here are a few more power words to consider:

Liaised – researched – analysed – controlled – supervised – represented – acknowledged – Instructed – coached – trained – briefed – encouraged – directed – rewarded – praised – motivated – assessed – delivered – designed – explained – prepared – promoted – participated – succeeded.

Writing the Cover Letter – Structure

Remember the 'top and tail' rule of writing letters. When writing to someone you have a name for you tail the letter with 'Yours sincerely'. If it's a 'Dear Sir or Madam' top, you tail with 'Yours faithfully'. Don't forget to add the date to the letter or email.

Use a clear font – Tahoma, Calibri, Century Gothic, Arial, Trebuchet MS or Candara at 12-point size. Some designs are easy to read at 11 point, like Century Gothic, if you have a lot to say. But try to write a stand-out half page and no more than a single A4 page. Check and double check your grammar and spelling, read and re-read your letter. Also, write a first draft then leave it, walk away and return to make sure you're happy with the contents before you hit the send button or seal the envelope. I bet you'll want to modify your text once you look at what you've written for a second time. Make each letter freshly written for each person. Try to make it personal to them and their company. Do your research. LinkedIn is a good resource for researching individuals, their current roles and backgrounds. Importantly, you must research the company and its products or services to be able to match your skills with their demands and their trading operation. This is so helpful in fashioning a letter that will leap out.

If you're sending your CV via email, copy and paste your letter (that you've have prepared in draft and checked beforehand) into the main body of the email so that it looks like a letter. Your CV will be added as an attachment. The template below is one example layout; check on the net to see if there are others that suit your purposes better.

Date

Person's name, company name and address   Your name and Address

Header in bold: **Job title you're applying for**   Your contact details

Please see my attached CV.

Dear Mr George/Miss George,

First Paragraph:

- State the reasons why you'd like to work for his/her particular company.
- State that you believe this position is the next step in your future career – the experience, the training, the development you'll receive to help you achieve your career ambitions.

Second Paragraph:

- State the contribution you will make to their success.
- State the reasons why you are suited to the position on offer – match your skills and talents with the job specification.

Final Paragraph:

- Round off with the business-related talents you possess, with a reference to your personality that touches on the nature of your character – your enthusiasm, your wish to develop skills, your commitment. Any relevant item in your private life that may crossover to this job scenario.

Sign off:

- I look forward to meeting you to explore this opportunity further.
- (Provide key contact details) You can reach me on Mobile/Cell xxxxx Email: me@myaddress.me

Yours sincerely

Signature (or email signature image)

You and only You (state name)

Your postal address (at bottom of page if email, top of page if a hard copy letter)

SECTION 4

HELPFUL REFERENCE

PUNCTUATION TIPS AND AN A TO Z OF USEFUL TERMS
MORE BRAIN FOOD

This section is designed to help your punctuation skills and provide explanations of some common business terms.

Punctuation – Punctuation Marks Decoded

The Full-Stop, Full-Point or Period
At the end of sentences:
The single dot of a full-stop marks the end of a sentence that doesn't end in an exclamation mark or question mark. The point at the bottom of these marks is the full stop that triggers an automatic capital letter in the next line when you're using a personal computer.

As 3 dots (known as ellipses):
When you see three full-stops together it means the reader is expected to complete the flow of text in their head, or that the writer has deliberately left a thought hanging for the reader to complete:

'The handcuffs snapped shut, the prisoner was dragged away never to return. With a backward sneer of undiluted venomous hatred Paul knew he could never count on it... '

Time:
No full-points for a modern look and no spaces: *am and pm, 3am/9pm.*

In one word sentences:
"Halt!" "Stop!" "No." "Goodbye."

Notice the full-point is directly after the word and 'inside' the speech marks. The use of the exclamation mark reinforces a command but has the same punctuation effect. When writing documents, it's a good idea to vary the length of sentences and often the abrupt use of just one word adds drama.

The Comma

Commas are staging points in a sentence. They allow the reader to take a heartbeat pause when faced with a long block of text, but they can also be used to add emphasis and stress to a piece. Commas can help to organise chunks of text into logical blocks. Essentially, the comma is best used to make sure the meaning of a sentence is clear. Here are some examples.

To organise actions or ideas in a block of similarity:
He entered the office, walked to the photocopier, turned on his computer, sat down and read his messages.

To organise nouns:
He picked up his pen, phone, briefcase and papers.

To add emphasis, sometimes linked to the use of adjectives:
His secretary was intelligent, helpful, considerate, stunningly attractive, painfully young and strictly off-limits.

To replace the use of brackets in a sentence:
The expert, having tried to solve the problem twice before, finally cracked the HTML code.

The Semicolon

The semicolon allows the writer to create a link between two separate sentences where the content is related. Semicolons are used when there is a common theme but separate points are being made, often in list form. The semicolon sends a different message from a comma. It alerts the reader that the direction of the sentence is about to change. Importantly, a semicolon can be used within a sentence as a punctuation substitute for conjunction words – and, or, but.

Examples of Semicolon Usage:
Where sentences are linked by a semicolon as a substitute for conjunctions (and, or, but):
The office was closed today; it will be open again next week.

A semicolon used to punctuate a list inside a sentence:

The Coen Brothers have been responsible for some of the most successful 'indie' films of recent times: The Big Lebowski; Fargo; Oh! Brother, Where Art Thou; Burn after Reading, *to name but a fabulous few.*

The Colon

The colon mark alerts the reader that a phrase or sentence is about to be extended, and is usually used before a list, a summary or quote. Here are some examples.

Before a list:
After work he made himself a Pina Colada: white rum, coconut cream and pineapple.

Before a summary:
To recap: the Mighty Word pre-Christmas campaign was an outstanding success.

Before a quote:
Mae West once said: "When choosing between two evils, I always like to try the one I've never tried before."

Dashes and Hyphens

Hyphens are punctuation marks that connect two or more words, like up-and-coming or door-to-door. Dashes have a weightier grammatical job of adding drama to a sentence, for example: *'He rushed into the meeting – it would be his last.'* Whether it is to add drama or join words the role is the same – to clarify understanding. Here are some uses:

1. Hyphens as pre-fixes to help word meaning:
   Re-visit Re-engineer Re-evaluate Re-read
2. Where the key word is capitalised:
   pre-Christmas anti-Nuclear anti-American
3. Where there is an established convention to qualify the noun:
   ex-wife vice-captain president-elect vice-chairperson
4. To avoid misunderstanding:
   're-present' – meaning to show again as opposed to 'represent' something or someone.
5. Where words have the same prefix or suffix:
   pre- and post-evaluation over- and under-prescribing
6. With fractions, such as:
   One-quarter one-half two-thirds Twenty-three sixty-four
7. When numbers clarify and define the adjective:
   40-hour working week 28-day cooling off period Twenty-first century technology
8. With words that start with a capital letter:
   X-ray T-shirt U-turn A-line
9. With compound adjectives that modify the word they precede:
   Up-to-date design Blue-chip account State-of-the-art development

Apostrophes: Before and after 'S'

The incorrect use of apostrophes is one of the most common punctuation headaches.

Apostrophes are the 'bad boys' of punctuation and have been saved for last for good reason. They cause the most bother and confusion, with people either using them wrongly or using them where they are not needed.

The apostrophe in 'shouldn't' is an example where an apostrophe is used to replace a missing letter, using the apostrophe to shorten a word. This is termed word contraction.

The Use of Apostrophes

1. Apostrophes used as word contractions:
    Contraction is the easiest concept to get your head around. Here are some more common contractions where an apostrophe replaces a missing letter, the contraction first then the original term:

Don't	*Do not*
It's	*It is or It has*
Wasn't	*Was not*
He's	*He is*
They're	*They are*

2. The Singular and Plural use of Apostrophes:
    The general rule is that when you are dealing with possession or ownership by an individual person or a single entity the apostrophe is marked BEFORE the S.

    Singular Possession: The Apostrophe is before the S
    Jack's car Jill's handbag John's teeth Julie's hair

    Singular Possession for nouns not ending in S – Add an 'S
    The rabbit's ears The child's clothes The hen's eggs

3. Apostrophes used when the possession is plural – Add an apostrophe AFTER the S.

    This is when talking about a group of people or things – i.e. in instances where the group is referred to as an entity of more than one, for example:
    The soldiers' duty – the duty of all the soldiers, as opposed to 'a soldier's

duty' – the duty of just one soldier

The rabbits' cage – the cage for all the rabbits – as opposed to 'the rabbit's cage' – the cage for just one rabbit

4. Using Apostrophes in common and uncommon possession:

   For common possession add an apostrophe S to the last name – as this couple are 'as one' and in common with each other, as in:

   Jack and Jill's house

   For uncommon possession:

   Barry's and Paul's houses – where Barry and Paul live in separate houses and as such are referred to separately

5. No Apostrophes Needed

   Apostrophes are not used where 'its' is a possessive statement, for example:

   The elephant flapped its ears. The bird fed its young. The club was pleased with its performance.

   Apostrophes are not used for plurals, for example in year numbers:

   70s, 80s, and 90s –or in these others too: *MPs, CDs, DVDs*

Spell Check

Commonly misspelt words – Spelt Correctly	
Accommodate	Liaison
Acknowledgement (UK spelling)	Liaise
Acknowledgment (USA spelling - no 'e' after g)	Occasion
	Occurrence
Argument	Perseverance
Commitment	Prerogative
Committed	Privilege
Consensus	Proceed
Deductible	Separate
Embarrass	Withhold
Existence	Targeted
Inadvertent	Definitely
Indispensable	Benefited

A-Z Directory of Useful Words and Terms

A.

AddThis: Is code that can be added to your site to allow users to share your content.

API: Application Programming Interface. A software application that allows contact with another application.

Avatar: An avatar is an image or username that represents a real person online in forum or social networks.

Affect and Effect: Affect is primarily used as a verb – 'the interview affected him greatly.' Effect is primarily used as a noun – 'the effect was tragic'.

Adverbs: Formed by adding 'ly' to an adjectives – bad = badly.

Adverbs are not nouns, for example – 'the footballer played brilliant' should be – 'played brilliantly'.

Acronyms: Some interesting ones here and throughout the A-Z Directory.

AIDA: Attention – Interest – Desire – Action

ABC: Always – Be – Closing (a sale)

ADDIE: Analysis – Design – Development – Implementation – Evaluation

Ampersand: The symbol '&' to mean 'and'.

Above-the-line: The 'line' being the line media agencies that are paid on a commission basis e.g. Advertising agencies, press, radio – and those that are paid on an agreed project fee basis e.g. Sales promotion agencies, PR and Direct Marketing.

B.

Blog: Is a web content publishing platform that posts news, updates and articles to promote a company's goods or services online. Blogger and WordPress are examples of blog platforms.

Bacronyms: letter meanings created to fit an existing word e.g. YAHOO = You Always Have Other Options

BING: Because It's Not Google

BID: Break It Down. When teaching/learning, break a concept/idea/problem down into manageable parts.

BOCCA: Belief – Optimism – Courage – Conviction –Action. Building blocks in the process of change.

Business Angel: A wealthy individual who is willing to invest in a high-risk start-up or small company but will demand a high percentage return, usually in equity and finance.

Benchmarking: Establishing a base-line to judge future performance, sometimes calculated by researching competitive activity.

C.

Crowdsourcing: The process of reaching out to gain connections with interested parties online, often to support a cause. This uses the feedback from the crowd to test ideas or reactions to a product or service.

Circles or Google Circles: Are online groupings of people that share similar interests or links.

Connections: Are people you join up with on online networking sites like Facebook or LinkedIn.

Capitalisation UK/Capitalization USA: The amount of money invested in the company in terms of cash, stocks/shares and bonds.

CLAMPS: Challenge – Location – Advancement –Money – Prestige – Security: Acronym from the Human Resources, Employment and Recruitment industries. These are the six acceptable reasons for leaving your last job.

Clicks and Bricks: A business strategy that involves both online and traditional retail sales.

D.

Digg: A content-sharing platform for pictures, views and videos.

Dependant: A noun – someone/something that depends upon someone/something.

Dependent : An adjective – meaning to be reliant on someone or something

Direct Mail: Using the delivery system of the mail/the post to reach your target audience in their home or place of work.

Direct Marketing: The whole range of different marketing options to promote a product or brand directly to a defined target market.

DAGMAR: Defined Advertising Goals (to)Measure Advertising Results.

E.

Engagement: The prime function of social media, to make and maintain contact and personal influence.

Entrepreneur: The French word for an innovator who goes it alone to set up and run a business.

e-business/e-commerce: The exchange/sale of goods and services via the internet

EDIP: Explain – Demonstrate – Imitate – Practice. A useful general teaching aid to encourage learning.

F.

Facebook: The world's most popular online networking platform for both family, social and business.

Fulfilment: To complete an order for despatch – also, the process of responding to customer queries/concerns.

FIFO: First In First Out. A form of stock/inventory control where the first stock received is rotated to be the first sold.

Foursquare: A location-based online search service that helps people find local places that are relevant to their interests.

G.

Google +: A more closely defined sharing platform for circles of interest. Google+ search algorithm takes into account the number and location of the people sharing content and has a direct impact on search engine results.

Gap Analysis: A favourite technique for examining the market to identify possible new product opportunities. It entails gathering information via consumer research and market appraisals to see if there is a 'gap' that can be filled to meet consumer/trade demand.

Gateway: An e-commerce term for where two or more computer networks meet to exchange information.

GLAM: Greying Leisured Affluent Married: Acronym from the market research industry, a socio-economic description.

GROW: Goals – Reality – Options – Will. This is a life-coaching template to prioritise needs and chart a path to achieving them.

H.

Hootsuite: A social media management system to track conversations and analyse response.

Hashtag: A hashtag is a word or phrase preceded by the # symbol to identify messages relating to a particular topic. Hashtags are used as shortcut addresses to Twitter accounts for viewing or posting messages.

Harvesting: When a company sells a product line or business to reap short-term benefit from a line which has a limited lifespan, or the practice of extracting as much profit from a product line at the end of its lifecycle with minimum sales and marketing outlay.

HIP: High Involvement Product. A marketing term for a purchase that requires a great deal of personal commitment and consideration, e.g. buying an expensive car

Handle: A Twitter term for the name you've chosen for your Twitter account.

I.

Instagram: A rapidly growing platform for sharing videos and pictures. Owned by Facebook.

Integrated marketing communications: The interweaving of different marketing and media disciplines to achieve stated objectives.

Infomercial or Advertorial: The technique of combining information with a selling message.

INSET: In-Service Education (and) Training. On-the-job training, in business, schools and colleges.

J.

JICNARS: Joint Industry Committee for National Readership Surveys. The body that runs the UK 'ABC' (Audit Bureau of Circulation) newspaper and magazine readership research that produces a breakdown by socio-economic groups.

JIT: Just in Time. Ordering system where businesses are geared up to re-ordering stock at the very last minute to avoid carrying expensive stockholdings.

K.

Klout: Is a site that measures the social influence of individuals on a range of social media platforms such as Facebook, Flickr, Twitter, YouTube and other platforms.

KPIs: Key Performance Indicators. A measure, standard or target used to judge performance based on past results or future expectations. KPIs are a judge of company/business effectiveness.

KISS: Keep It simple and Straightforward

KEY: Keep Extending Yourself. Another personal/business coaching acronym to reinforce the need to keep moving forward, learning new skills and maintaining development.

L.

LIBOR: London Inter-Bank Offered Rate, the setter for the UK wholesale money-lending rate between banks to balance their books on a daily basis.

Leveraged Buyout: The acquisition of a company using borrowed funds in the expectation of repaying the debt out of funds generated by the acquired company.

Laissez-faire: The doctrine or system of Government non-interference in the economy.

LIP: Low Involvement Product. The opposite of HIP – no real thought or consideration is needed prior to purchase.

M.

Macroeconomics: A branch of economics that deals with national and international economic issues like national income and national expenditure.

Microeconomics: Economics geared to examining the behaviour of individuals or small groups of people.

Marketable: A product judged to have commercial potential.

Marketing mix: A combination of product, packaging, promotion, publicity and price geared to creating a strong bedrock for the launch or further exploitation of a product or service.

MBO: Management By Objectives. Coaching and training geared to help an individual achieve corporate objectives.

MBO: Acronym used to mean Management Buy Out.

N.

NASDAQ: National Association of Securities Dealers Automated Quotations. Set up in 1971, this is a computer-screen based securities trading system.

Nikkei 225: Japan's price weighted index of the Tokyo Stock Exchange.

NYSE: New York Stock Exchange. Set up in 1789 when George Washington authorised the issue of $80 million in Government bonds to help finance the War of Independence:

NB: *Nota-Bene*, the Italian phrase to draw attention to a particular point of importance in a document; the literal translation of *Nota Bene* is 'observe well'

O.

OHO: Only Here Once. Reason for becoming involved or rationale for taking a risk

Oligopoly: Where a few companies control the greatest % of sales

Obsolescence: The decline of a product due to the threat from newer, improved products. Built-in obsolescence is a policy of designing a product with an artificially limited useful life, so it will become obsolete after a certain period of time. Outsourcing: The transfer of internal jobs/tasks to external contractors.

P.

Prezi: Is highly flexible presentation software. Prezumes are personal CVs or resumes created using Prezi software.

Pinterest: A photo and information sharing site, the idea being to 'Pin' your piece to a global pin-board.

Privatisation (UK) or Privatization (USA): The process of selling Government-owned assets to the private sector.

Price discrimination: The practice of selling the same item to different customers at different prices – both to national and international markets.

Psychographics: The technique used to describe market behaviour using personal attitudinal data, lifestyle, occupation, age, interests, ethnicity and sex.

PAY: Prioritise Activities (by) Yield. The method of evaluation that judges effective action by the end result – a 'work smarter' technique.

PIMS: Profit Impact (of) Marketing Strategy. A reminder that profit is always the ultimate objective of any marketing initiative.

Q.

Questionnaire (note double 'n' spelling): A Q&A information-gathering form used in marketing research.

Quantitative easing: The injection of quantities of cash into the financial system to give banks extra capital. The increased supply of cash is designed to trigger a greater release of loans to businesses and individuals.

QUANGO: Quasi Autonomous Non-Governmental Organisation

QED: From the Latin *quod-erat-demonstrandum*, meaning 'the proposition has been proved'.

Qualified Lead: The qualifying of a sales lead from an outside prospect to a likely sales conversion. This is normally established through research and personal contact to assess the chance of a sale.

R. Retweet: The process by which Twitter tweets are forwarded to others to dramatically increase the reach of comment and information. Often shortened to RT. Random sampling: An unbiased sampling technique in which all people contacted have an equal chance of being represented in a research project, as opposed to being open only to a particular niche market. Response marketing: An e-marketing term for the management of a prospect from the time contact is first made through to final sale conversion. Rate-of-Return: The arithmetical calculation of the relationship between the cost of a project and the financial benefit generated.
S. ShareThis: A code that can be added to a website to make sharing of content easier on social media channels. Sales Promotion: Can be defined as giving 'Temporary Added Value' to provide an incentive to purchase or participate. Sales promotion uses a variety of techniques termed heavyweight or lightweight based on cost vs. impact. Money-off is the most costly with the greatest impact but does not improve product image or perception. SEO: Search-Engine-Optimisation. The skill of marketing a website to attract search engines and boost rankings to gain more website visitors.
T. Twitter: Social media platform for sharing short messages up to 140 characters long. Target Market: An identified specific group of either consumer or trade customers. A combination of socio-economic and personal interest factors narrow down those people who are most likely to become involved with a product or service. Microtargeting is segmenting individuals into ever more closely defined interests and behaviour patterns to include street-by-street analysis in a community as well as personal preferences.
U. USP: Unique Selling Proposition(or Plus): The single key benefit of your product/service that makes it stand out from the competition. UPB: Unique Perceived Benefit. The flipside of 'USP' that looks at your product/service through the eyes of consumers and asks what appeals to them about your product/service.

V.

Viral Marketing: Using online marketing techniques to promote a business, product or person, including email, blogging and social networking and business networking channels.

Vimeo: A platform for sharing video content, such as YouTube

W.

White Knight: A company that is subject to an unwelcome/hostile bid or takeover approach may search for an alternative company or business that is more acceptable to them – a White Knight

Web marketing: SEO and online marketing to promote products and services online aimed at focusing attention on a website for customer conversion

---

X.

XML: Xtensible Mark-up Language. An electronic code for documents in textual data format designed for use on the internet.

Xing: A European professional network.

Y.

YouTube: A video sharing platform owned by Google and important as a part of an online marketing strategy to complement other SEO activity.

Yamma: A closed communication network within one organisation or company or private groups.

Z.

Zeebox: An app that creates a social media dashboard from mobile and pc to register the interaction between your television watching and social media habits.

Please visit
www.transformyourskills.com
For the latest news and blogs

Other books by the author:

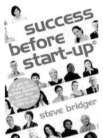

SUCCESS BEFORE START UP

www.successbeforestartup.co.uk

Success before Start Up shares the start-up experiences of 19 small businesses. It covers the human factor, marketing, finance and business planning. These are the 'Four Factors of Start-Up Success'. The human factor being the most important of all. The idea behind *Success before Start Up* is to make you aware of the most common pitfalls of starting a new business and how to avoid crashing and burning in the first vital months. The book describes the seven most popular types of business and helps you choose which type is right for you. By reading this book you'll be better prepared to make your business a success.

Paperback ISBN 978 19082 18759
Mobipocket/Kindle: 978 19802 18766 epub ISBN: 978 19082 18773

ONE DEGREE NORTH
Escape to an exotic world of danger and intrigue

Welcome to the exotic island of Singapore, one degree north of the equator. It's February 1965, the second year of a small war: the Indonesian Confrontation. Communist insurgents are mounting ever increasing attacks on civilian targets and challenging the security forces. The criminal underworld is being challenged too. These attacks are bad for business. Takings from gambling, prostitution, opium dens and protection rackets are down. Enter a beautiful but deadly femme fatale to really spice things up.

Plotting, deception, murder and intrigue rule the dark side of this tropical island paradise. You don't expect MI6 and the CIA to stand by and do nothing, do you? Remember the saying: All's fair in love and war.

Paperback ISBN: 978 1907798 597
Mobipocket/Kindle ISBN: 978 1907798 603 epub ISBN: 978 1907798 610